Mooschie G Daniel

Modern Persia

Mooschie G Daniel

Modern Persia

ISBN/EAN: 9783743316867

Manufactured in Europe, USA, Canada, Australia, Japa

Cover: Foto ©ninafisch / pixelio.de

Manufactured and distributed by brebook publishing software
(www.brebook.com)

Mooschie G Daniel

Modern Persia

ODERN PERSIA

[illegible]

[illegible]

فی معلم موسی کورکیس دانیال

ملتم نصاری وطنم ارومی

MODERN PERSIA

BY

RABBI MOOSHIE G. DANIEL,

McCORMICK SEMINARY

Late Professor of Ancient Syriac in Oroomiah College, Persia.

ܪܒܝ ܡܘܫܐ ܓܝܘܪܓܝܣ ܕܒܝܬ ܕܢܝܐܝܠ :

ܐܠܐ ܕܐܘܪܡܝ: ܘܡܫܝܚܐ ܕܡܫܝܚܝܐ.

فی معلّم موسای گورگس دانیال

ملّتم نصاری وطنم ارومی

TORONTO:

HENDERSON & COMPANY

1898

TO THE

CLASS OF 1897

OF

McCORMICK THEOLOGICAL SEMINARY,

AND TO

REV. DR. CAVEN OF KNOX COLLEGE, TORONTO,

WHOSE FINE MISSIONARY SPIRIT AND GREAT KINDNESS ARE MUCH APPRECIATED, THIS VOLUME IS RESPECTFULLY DEDICATED BY THE AUTHOR.

PREFACE.

THE author, in spending four years in America, has come in contact with different classes of people who have raised serious questions concerning modern Persia.

Those who are interested in politics and government, have asked: Is modern Persia a province of Turkey? Is it as large as the State of Michigan? Is the king still absolute, as in ancient times? Have the laws of the Medes and Persians undergone no change? Are there any remains of Persia's ancient beauty and grandeur?

These, and questions like these, have been from time to time presented to the author. On the other hand it is to be observed that many journalists traveling through Persia have greatly misrepresented that country. Their limited stay made it impossible for them to acquire any accurate knowledge of the country.

It is no easy task to familiarize oneself with the ideas and customs of that ancient and historic country. To thousands in Persia the literature and history of their own land is a sealed book.

Questions the most serious and earnest have been raised by godly ministers and devoted people who have for years been generous givers to the cause of Foreign Missions. I have been asked questions like these: Is there a solid foundation established by missions in Persia? What has the Gospel done? What changes have taken place? What are some of the fruits of our mission work over there? What are some of the temporal improvements? Very recently Rev. O. N. Hunt of Edwardsburg, Mich., wrote the author asking what is the moral condition of Persia to-day in comparison to what it was when the missionaries began their work?

Questions like these prompted the author to write this small book.

Its object is to encourage the mission spirit; to quicken and kindle anew the fires of divine love in the hearts of all those to whom it will come; to promote and advance the blessed Gospel of our Lord and His Christ; to hasten the day when millions that now sit in darkness and the shadow of death may set their faces toward the light.

Oh, Jehovah of the East!
Who was once born in the East,
Who preached and was crucified in the East,
When wilt thou again visit the East?

Remarks: The author wishes to say that, in the survey of modern Persia, free use was made of the International Encyclopedia, especially in the matter of dates.

Dr. Philip Schaff's Church History was also consulted in the account given of Mohammed.

The leaves of the trees are the gift of the poor.

INTRODUCTION.

THIS book is by a native, who knows at first-hand of what he writes. He writes of those features and facts of Persia as a country and a people in which an intelligent American is most sure to be interested. Very ancient and renowned among the Asiatics, Persia, persisting in her nationality and gradually improving her condition excites enquiry abroad. In this volume we have a view of her geographical divisions, her form of government, system of taxation, methods of merchandise, educational conditions and the state of religion.

The author also particularizes and portrays the character, creed and course of Mohammed: how Moslemism was propagated by violence and perpetuated by deceit, and of such false doctrines as hatred toward enemies, and rewards in heaven and hell. The reader is informed of Bobeism, a new sect which has arisen in opposition to government and orthodox Mohammedanism. The book was written for the reading public, and by its style, movement and contents is calculated not only to enlarge one's general knowledge of the land of the Shah, but to quicken interest in the enterprise of Christian Missions, which are the chief hope of the country.

REV. JOHN L. WITHROW, D.D., LL.D.

Ex-Moderator of General Assembly.
Chicago, Ill., July 19, '97.

Mr. Mooshie G. Daniel is an excellent representative of the Syrian nationality and the Nestorian Church. He has completed his course of study in McCormick Theological Seminary, and it is his purpose to return to Persia, his native country, as a missionary. His little work on Persia is quite interesting, and is written with full knowledge of all matters of which it treats. The author first wrote part of it in Persian, and with the assistance of fellow-students has rendered it into good English. It contains information not readily accessible to most, and is pervaded by a fine spirit. The beliefs and practices of the religious sects of Persia are described with the intimate knowledge of one who is a native of the country, and has given special attention to the subject. Mr. Daniel's little book has received commendation from excellent judges.

REV. WM. CAVEN, D.D., LL.D.
Principal Knox College.

Toronto, 23rd June, 1898.

CONTENTS.

PAGE.

Life of Mooshie G. Daniel in Persia. . 13-20

Life of Mooshie G. Daniel in America. 21-23

PART I.

CHAPTER.

I. General Survey of Persia—Climate and Products—Inhabitants — Manufactories and Trades — Government and Taxation—The Army. . . . 25-30

II. The Ancient History of Persia. 30-38

III. Architecture of Persia 39-43

IV. The Language and Poetry of Persia 44-50

PART II.

Religions.

I. Parsee Religion—Bible and Doctrines—Their Rituals. . . . 51-58

II. Mohammedanism — Mohammed —His Birth and Character— The Conquest of Islam. . . . 58-67

III. The Mohammedan Religion. . 68-69

IV. The Creed of Islam. 70-71

V. The Priesthood — Mujtahids — Arch - Mujtahids, Common Mujtahids — Mollah — The Sayyids—Darwishes — Their Service. 71-84
VI. The Laymen—Middle Class—Low Class 84-90
VII. The Mosques and their Services —Special Service. 91-95
VIII. Moslem's Private Prayer and Fasting. 95-99
IX. The Pilgrimages — Preparation —Almsgiving—Carrying the Dead — The Motive in Pilgrimages for the Dead—The Female Pilgrims—Their Returning. 100-10
X. The Shiite Moslem's Mu-har-ram —Singers. 110-20
XI. Heaven and Hell 121-24
XII. Matrimony. 124-29

PART III.

I. The Royal Family—The King in His Palace — His Table— Treasury—Wives. 129-37
II. Governor — Prisons — Executions. 137-43
III. Counts or Lords. 143-45
IV. Cities, Schools and Holidays . 145-53

PART IV.

I. Bobeism—Bobe—His Doctrine —His Personal Appearance . 154-61
II. The Kurds—Occupation—Their Character — Houses — Religion. 162-68

PART V.

I. The Nestorians—Their Place—Language. 169-71
II. Their History 172-73
III. Clergy 173-74
IV. Churches and Ordinances . . 175-79
V. Assyrian or Nestorian College . 179-80
VI. Assyrian Missionary Spirit . 184-86
VII. Their Persecutions . . . 186-91
VIII. Their Condition at the Time American Missions were Started 191-92

PART VI.

I. Introduction of Mission Work 193-95
II. Method of Work 195-98
III. Development of Mission Work. 199-202
IV. Religious Education—College—Ladies' Seminary—Medical Schools—Country Schools—Translation of Books . 202-212

V. The Gospel and Temporal Improvement — Temperance — Conversion to Mohammedanism—Morals Elevated . . 213-221
VI. Mission Work Among Moslems . 222-223

LIFE OF MOOSHIE G. DANIEL IN PERSIA.

THE ancestors of M. G. Daniel, a true stock of the Nestorian sect and Syrian nationality, came down from Kurdiston mountain in 1740 and settled in Persia at Oroomiah district. The one family, now increased to fifty, all live in villages near to each other. G. Daniel, with his four brothers, settled in a small village four miles east of Oroomiah city. The inhabitants of this village are composed of fifty Mohammedan families and twenty-eight Nestorians. His parents had four sons and two daughters, all died in their childhood. Daniel was their seventh child, born in 1861. His native village was visited by Rev. G. Coan, D.D., and Dr. Perkins, missionaries from America, who preached the Gospel message to the Nestorians of that village, at the same time also started a school for their children. At this time Daniel was thirteen years old. The parents were very glad to send their children to this school, which increased to thirty students.

Daniel was very anxious to attend this school. This desire was encouraged in every possible way by his earnest, self-sacrificing Christian mother, Rachel, who came of high and noble lineage. But his father vigorously objected for fear his son would change from his old Nestorian faith. When Daniel saw other boys going to school he would often cry and pray that God would change his father's heart and lead him to send his son to school. This sincere desire on the part of the young and ardent lad led to an earnest discussion and difference between his parents as to the future policy with their boy. Finally, after two months' fervent prayer on the part of the mother and her son, the Spirit of God reconciled the opposition of the father and made him willing to send his son to school. Daniel continued his studies in this school four years, and read a chapter of the Bible to his parents every night. The father thus became interested, and in the second year sent Daniel's two sisters and brother to school. He soon became the first student in the school. Rev. G. Coan, when visiting the school, embraced Daniel and his sisters and kissed them with the holy kiss of joy as the first-fruit of his labors.

After four years this school closed on account of lack of students. There arose a dark cloud of sorrow and disappointment to poor Daniel. What shall I do to continue my studies, was the despairing cry of the consecrated boy. But his strong will soon found a way. He was now sixteen years old. There was a small village of three hundred families called Golpashan two miles distant from his home town. Golpashan contained a high school and a Presbyterian church of three hundred members. Daniel decides to go to school at this place, but again meets opposition from his father, who wants him to stay at home and work for him. But his mother met his father with the strong argument that she had consecrated her child to God before he was born, "because God gave him to me after the death of my six children." But the mother lived in continual fear that her son would be devoured by wolves on his way to school, and then she said, "I will go down to my grave in a miserable condition." But the son, willing to sacrifice even life itself for study, said, "I will go, mother, trusting in God and your prayers." Events soon proved that the mother's fears were well founded. Once, very early in the morning, while on his way to school he was attacked by a large, ferocious wolf, but he made good his escape up a tree near by. He received such a shock from this attack that he was prostrated three months, and his life was despaired of by all his friends. But God graciously restored him to health for His holy ministry. Daniel always believed in the outstretched hand of God that snatched him from the wolf. Hundreds of times he thanks God in his prayers for this deliverance.

When Mr. Daniel was seventeen years old he reached the greatest crisis of his life. His parents decided to marry him to a girl a few steps only from his residence, because the parents of the couple had decided when they were children to marry them to each other. This was in accordance with a foolish custom of the Nestorians. His father had firmly decided to make the match, but his mother said, "Only if he himself wishes." But Daniel's aim was very high; he was running to obtain a higher prize. He said to his mother, "I am married to my studies." His mother replied, "My son, I have dedicated you to God, I cannot compel you to marry." His father was full of indignation and anger against the disobedience of his son, and he said, "I will never send you to the Presbyterian college. I cannot spend one cent on you."

Daniel was very fond of fishing, hunting, and raising grapes, and was one of the best husbandmen in Persia. One morning when fishing a young man whose name was Abraham, and afterward a classmate for seven years in college, handed to him an envelope in which was written by Dr. Oldfather, a missionary, and President of the Presbyterian College at Oroomiah, Persia, "We havè accepted you in our college." Daniel thought this a calling from Jesus Christ, just as He had called four of His disciples from their fishing. He threw his net on the shore of the river, and, kneeling down, thanked God for this, His holy calling. Rising up from his prayer, he took his net and started for home. On arrival he told his parents that he wanted to go to college. Again his father objected, saying that he could not spend any money for his education.

But his mother sold all her jewels and sent him to college.

COLLEGE LIFE.

In 1875 Daniel went to Oroomiah College. For first two years Rev. Dr. Oldfather was President of the college. In the second year he was converted by hearing a sermon and a song by Dr. Oldfather, whose singing quickens sleeping souls of sinners. His class at the beginning was thirty persons, but at graduation only twelve. He studied very hard, sitting up at night with his book until eleven o'clock. One of his classmates, Rev. Abraham, was his bosom friend. They recited in a small closet often until midnight and then had prayers before going to bed. Daniel graduated in 1882 under the presidency of Dr. J. H. Shedd, one of the most eminent men ever sent as a missionary to Persia by the Presbyterian Church. All his classmen are leaders in the Presbyterian Church as well as of the Nestorian nation, for two of them have lately been offered the title "count" by the late Shah. Dr. S. J. Alamsha, a noble, consecrated Doctor of Medicine, one of the fellow-graduates of Daniel, shows the tenor of the spirit of Christian fortitude and devotion in declaring his faith in the Trinity in the very face of the Governor of State, who had just threatened him with persecution by cutting off his hands if he insisted on repeating the confession. But Dr. Alamsha replied that he was a Christian, and if ever questioned as to his faith would confess it not only at the cost of his hands, but his head also. He further stated that he would not impose his faith on any one unless they requested, and that if the Governor did not want his confession he had better not ask for it.

Two weeks after Daniel's graduation he was elected instructor in the high school for three years. Each year he had a week of revival meetings, which was very fruitful in the conversion of many students. Nearly one hundred students were graduates under him in high school. In 1885 Daniel was married to Miss

WIFE AND DAUGHTER OF THE AUTHOR.

Sarah George, a young lady graduate of the Ladies' Seminary, whose mother was instructor in this seminary for seven years. In 1886 was offered to him the chair of Ancient Syriac in Oroomiah College, which he occupied for seven years. His many friends rejoiced with him in his call to this higher and wider field of labor. When he moved to college, Mrs. Daniel was very ambitious for his success in college. She said, "I like to tell you I want you to teach your studies better than any professor in the college; I want you to devote all your time to your work; I want you to be a shining example to all students; I want you to love all students as your brothers; I want you to respect yourself. Be kind to all students; let our home be as their homes. I want you to preach the best sermons; then you will be the crown of my head, and I will love you as the pupil of my eyes." This was a very hard charge, and very precious work, but it proved for Daniel very precious jewels. Mrs. Daniel is one of the most intelligent ladies of Persia. For the first three years he went to bed always at eleven o'clock, and taught each week twenty-six studies. Three times a week he conducted Gospel meetings, and each alternate Sabbath conducted Sabbath school. He was a leader of the college church, secretary of Board of Education, Superintendent and Quester of County schools. The testimony of Faculty and Board of Education was that he taught ancient Syriac better than any of his predecessors. Daniel was the youngest member of the Faculty. He had students ten years older than himself, but they all loved him as their brother. Sometimes he would spend as much as two hours a night talking and praying with individual students. Four months of winter for several years he was visitor of the county schools. Besides this he worked in revival meetings during one week in his own church. While working with the pastor he preached twice each day, and forty-two persons were converted. When he was leaving town all elders, deacons and other prominent men escorted him a long distance with much gratitude. His piety and integrity were taken as an example by Christian and non-Christian.

LIFE OF MOOSHIE G. DANIEL IN AMERICA.

CHURCH, SCHOOL AND CLASS.

ON the first of October, 1895, I entered McCormick Seminary. Immediately feeling the need of identifying myself with the church, I accordingly became a member of the Church of the Covenant, Dr. W. S. Plummer Bryan, pastor. It is impossible to set down in words the comfort, encouragement and assistance that has come to me through this relation. Dr. Bryan has been to me a steadfast and faithful friend. His sermons have been to me a continual source of instruction in things spiritual and Divine. Many of them have left a lasting impression upon my mind. One I remember with great distinctness. It was upon the last seven words of Christ; so real and vivid did the scene appear that the whole of that mournful tragedy was enacted before my eyes. Concerning the Church of the Covenant, I can say with David, "If I forget thee, O Jerusalem, let my right hand forget her cunning. If I do not remember thee, let my tongue cleave to the roof of my mouth, if I prefer not Jerusalem above my chief joy." Even though I were on the other side of the globe, I will not forget the kindness of the church and its pastor.

Naturally my life at the seminary at first was lonesome; but as soon as I became acquainted with professors and students the seminary became a home to me much prized and enjoyed. From my studies I derived much pleasure. Systematic Theology was to me a continual banquet of delicacies. In Pastoral Theology and Homiletics I was inspired with the high and sacred duties of the Christian ministry.

By the study of Greek Exegesis I was taught the invaluable benefit that comes from close attention to the original texts and manuscripts which are the source of interpretation in the study of New Testament Greek. In Old and New Testament literature belief in inspiration was reinforced and fortified. The whole scheme of the Christian religion was to me rendered plain and reasonable.

MY CLASS.

The class of 1897 is unique and original among all the classes graduated from McCormick Seminary. It was said by one in position to know that it was perhaps the strongest class ever sent out from the Seminary. This was evidenced by the character of the orations delivered at the graduating exercises. Among this class are many who will be adorned by degrees and honorary titles. All, I hope, will meet with much success in winning souls to Christ.

In personal appearance there are among them princes and lords; but one thing made me sorry every time I looked upon their faces, namely, that so many shaved their mustaches. My advice to all of them is to raise mustaches, and not appear like girls, but as princes. Some of them had such long and difficult names that I could not pronounce them, but a few had very easy names, for instance Mr. McGaughey, which means in Persian language, "Don't say so," a phrase used by young girls. Mr. Earhart, which means in ancient Syriac, "I will run." Mr. Ross in Arabic means "head." My class was very loving and kind to us two Persians. Every time we made good recitations in classes they were gladder than we were, and when we failed they became even more sorry than we. I remember once failing in my recitation, and after class Mr. Earhart came into my room to comfort me. The memories of my class are to me like sweet spices, and will be cherished by me everywhere I go.

PART I.

CHAPTER I.

GENERAL SURVEY OF PERSIA.

ONCE, in ages long past, Persia was the home of heroes, and was studded with palaces of splendor. Bards and poets of all nations have vied with each other in singing of the bravery of her sons and the beauty of her daughters. The names of Cyrus the Great, Darius and others are engraved in ever-living letters on the pages of history.

To-day, though her glory has flown away and her splendor has faded, her natural beauty remains untarnished. The words of the poet Sahdy are still true: "It is a paradise, making men drunken with the odors of its roses; it is a garden whose streams wreath the faces of men in smiles."

In 1826, in the war between Persia and Russia, the territory of the former was greatly reduced. It now contains 628,000 square miles, or three times the number in France or Germany. It is divided into thirteen states, as follows: Ghilon, Mazandaron, Ostorobad, in the north; Azerbijon, Persian Kurdistan, Luriston and Khuziston on the west; Fariston, Loriston, Kerman, with Mogiston, in the south; Irakeston, the capital state, where the king resides, being in the centre. On the east lies the large State of Khorason, which is mainly desert.

Persia is dotted with many great and small mountains, interspersed with fertile valleys, flowing fountains and silvery streams. Dense jungles abound in the States of Mazandaron and Ghilon.

CLIMATE AND PRODUCTS.

The great extent of the country gives rise to an extremely varied climate. Cyrus said of it: "The people perish with the cold at one extremity, while they are suffocated with the heat at the other." Persia may be considered to possess three climates: that of southern Dash tiston; of the elevated plateau; and of the Caspian provinces.

In Dashtiston the autumnal heats are excessive, those of summer are more tolerable, while in winter and spring the climate is delightful. In the plateau the climate of Fariston is temperate. About Isphahon, in the same plateau, the winters and summers are equally mild, and the regularity of the seasons appears remarkable to a stranger. The Caspian provinces, from their general depression below the level of the sea, are exposed to fierce heat during the summer months, though their winters are mild. Heavy rains are frequent, and many of the low districts are marshy and unhealthy. Except in the Caspian and northwest provinces, the atmosphere of Persia is remarkable above that of all other countries for its dryness and purity.

The cultivated portions of Persia, where there is a good rainfall or the land can be irrigated, produce an immense variety of crops. Here is grown the best wheat in the world. Other characteristic products are barley, rice, cotton, sugar and tobacco. Vineyards are plentiful. The vines of Shiroz are celebrated in Eastern poetry. Mulberries and silk are two other famous Persian products, while the finest perfumes are made from the countless varieties of roses, with which the land is carpeted.

The forests of the Elburz mountains abound with wild animals, such as wolves, tigers, jackals, wild boars, foxes and the Caspian cat. Deer of every variety inhabit some of the mountains. Lions and leopards are also found in Mazandaron. Among domestic animals the horse, the camel and the buffalo hold first place. The horses of Persia have always been celebrated as the finest in the East. They are larger and more handsome, but are not so fleet as the horses of Arabia. Sheep are one of the main sources of wealth of the country. All the rivers are well stocked with fish, especially with sturgeon. Silver, lead, iron, copper, salt, antimony, sulphur and naphtha are mined in large quantities. The late Shah found a little gold, but not in quantities sufficient to pay for mining.

INHABITANTS.

In the days of Darius and Cyrus the population numbered not less than 40,000,000, but that number has diminished until now not more than 10,000,000 people dwell in this once populous land. These are from different nationalities: the Kurds, numbering 500,000; Arabs, 500,000; Jews, 20,000; Nestorians, 60,000; Armenians, 60,000 ; Zoroastrians, 15,000, and the remainder are a Mohammedan sect.

MANUFACTORIES AND TRADES.

The manufactories of Persia are by no means extensive, but Persian rugs and shawls have a reputation the world over. The deft fingers of the women have contributed for centuries to the glory and wealth of this country. In the marts and markets of the world these rugs and shawls sell for fabulous prices. At the World's Fair I saw a single rug valued at $15,000.

Trade, both domestic and foreign, is carried on by caravans. Tabriz is the chief commercial city, and from this point goods to the value of $2,500,000 are exported annually. From the Province Shiraz about $900,000 worth of opium is sent out each year.

GOVERNMENT AND TAXATION.

The government of Persia is a pure despotism. The Shah is absolute monarch; he appoints governors for each of the thirteen states, and these governors, in turn, appoint minor governors for the cities. Six cabinet officers assist the executive, but their function is wholly advisory. Upon the least pretext any member of the cabinet may, at the will of the Shah, lose his head.

The country has been impoverished for ages from two principal sources. Nomadic tribes, wandering bands of Kurds and Arabs swoop down upon some unprotected villages and carry away everything of any value. Taxation is the second cause of poverty. The burden of the taxes falls upon Jews and Christians, the most cruel extortions often being used to obtain the desired amount. In 1882 the revenue was about £1,880,000, of which nearly £1,500,000 were from direct taxations. But notwithstanding so much is collected, not one cent goes for public improvements.

THE ARMY.

The standing army numbers about 130,000, of which only 30,000 are well-disciplined infantry, 10,000 artillery, 10,000 cavalry, and irregular infantry and guards constitute the remainder. The officers in the Persian army are for the most part ignorant and inefficient, while the soldiers are described as obedient, sober, intelligent and capable to endure great fatigue. The peculiar power of the Persian army lies in its irregular cavalry of Kurds and other tribes, who are famous for their courage and daring, and are equal to the Russian Cossacks, and vastly superior to the Turkish Sultan's Boshi-bozouks.

CHAPTER II.

THE ANCIENT HISTORY OF PERSIA.

According to the poet, Firdusi, in his "Shah Nomeh," the history of Persia begins some thousands of years before the Christian era. Professor Yooseph, of Oroomiah College, one of Persia's most scholarly men, holds that as early as the time of Abraham there was here an organized government. The first king

PERSIAN OFFICER.

was the Chedolaomer of the Bible, King of Elam (Gen. 14 : 1). This opinion is confirmed by the fact that the name Elam is in reality the name of Persia. Persians call their country Ajam. Thus it can be seen that the Hebrew letter l has been changed to j. However, there is stronger proof of this theory in the accounts of Greek historians. The northwest part of ancient Persia, called Media, was known to the Greeks as a part of the Assyrian Empire. But the Medes, under Dejoce in 708 B.C., threw off the yoke of Assyria, and gained the dominance over the other tribes of Persia. In 538 Cyrus of Persia rebelled against the Medes, led an army to victory over them, and extended the Persian Empire as far east as the Oxus and Indus and over Asia Minor, Syria, Palestine and Mesopotamia. He was succeeded by his son, Cambyses (529-522), and the latter by Darius (522-521). This dynasty ruled till Darius III. (336-329). He was compelled to yield his throne to Alexander the Great, who conquered all Persia. Under the leadership of the tribe of Arsocide, Persia became independent in 246 B.C. But the dynasty of Arsocide came to an end at the hand of Ardasher Babajan, who managed to gain possession of more than half of the entire country, *i.e.*, of the Provinces of Fars, Kerman and the whole of Irakiston.

Then in 218 this valiant warrior conquered the whole nation, and was crowned "King of Kings" (in Persian, Shah in Shah). With Ardasher began the famous dynasty of the Sassanide, who brought Persia to an unprecedented eminence of power and prosperity. Their last king succumbed to the Arabs in 636 A.D., and the latter ruled till 750 A.D. The tribe of the Abbossides went to the throne at this time, but were soon in turn overthrown. Persia was then divided into different provinces, until in 1253 it was conquered by the Mongols under Genghis-Khan and his grandson, Khulakun-Khan. The former was a Christian. During his reign Moryaw-Alaha was the Nestorian patriarch, and under him the Church was very successful. The Mongol dynasty lasted until 1335.

A new dynasty arose in western Persia in 1500. The first prince of this line was Ismael, the descendant of an ancient family of devotees and saints. He was held in the highest esteem by his followers, who revered him, not only on account of his own valor, but for the high standing of his family. Having become the leader of a number of tribes, he overthrew the power of the Turkoman and made Azerbijon their capital. He then rapidly subdued western Persia, and in 1511 took Khorason and Balkh from the Uzbeks. In the year 1514 he encountered a far more formidable enemy in the mighty Salim, sultan of Turkey, whose zeal for conquest was fanned by religious hatred of the Shiites, who were followers of Ismael, and who in turn were fiercely inflamed against a sect called Sunites. In the ensuing conflict Ismael was defeated, but Salim did not gain greatly by his victory. The son of Ismael, Shah Tahmasip, who reigned from 1523-1576, subdued all the Uzbeks of Khorason, and frequently defeated the Turks without suffering the loss of a single battle. He takes rank as a prudent and spirited ruler.

Shah Abbos I, the great, who was one of the most glorious of Persia's modern kings, ascended the throne in 1585, and ruled until 1628. He restored internal tranquillity and repelled the invasions of the Uzbeks and Turks. In the year 1605, he gave the Turks such a terrific drubbing that they made no more trouble during his long reign. He also restored to his kingdom Kurdiston-Mosul and Diarbekir which had long been separated from Persia. Abbos' government was strict, but just and equitable. Roads, bridges, caravansories, and other conveniences for trade were constructed at great cost, and the improvement and ornamentation of the towns were not neglected. Many of his large caravansories which bear his name remain to this day. Isphahan, his capital, in a brief period of his reign, doubled its population. His tolerance was remarkable, considering the character of his ancestors and subjects, for he encouraged the Armenian Christians to settle in the country, well knowing that their peaceable, industrious habits would enhance the prosperity of his kingdom. His successors were Shah Sufi (1628-41), Shah Abbos II. (1641-66) and Shah Soliman (1666-94). During the reign of Shah Sultan Hussein (1694-1722), a weak and foolish prince, priests and slaves were elevated to high offices, and the Sun-nites suffered sore persecution. The result was that Afghan beseiged the king in Isphahan. Hussein abdicated the throne in favor of his conqueror, who ultimately became insane and suffered deposition in 1725 at the hands of his brother, Ashrab. The atrocious tyranny of Ashrab was suddenly checked by the celebrated Nadir-Shah. Hussein and Ashrab belonged to the dynasty of Syydes, a holy sect, descendants of their prophet Mohammed. Nadir-Shah was one of the greatest warriors of Persia. He raised Tah-Masip (1729-32) and his son Abbos III. (1732-36), of the Suffivian race, to the throne, and then on some frivolous pretext deposed Abbos III. and seized the scepter himself (1736-47). Nadir

KING KARIM KHAN KURD.

was assassinated by Imam-Kuli-Khan, of Oroomiah, whose descendants now live very near our Mission Station in Oroomiah. Again, after the murder of Nadir, Persia was divided into many independent states, and became a field of blood. Bloogiston and Afghaniston became independent till 1755, when a Kurd, Karim Khan (1755-79), abolished this state of affairs, re-established peace and unity in western Persia, and by his justice, wisdom and warlike talents acquired both the esteem of his subjects and the respect of the neighboring states. He received the title, "Father of Persia." Karim Khan was succeeded in 1784 by Al-Murad, then by Jaafor and the latter by Lutf-Ali-Merza.

During Lutf-Ali's reign, Mazandaron became independent under Agha Mohammed Khan, a Turkoman. Lutf-Ali-Merza rushed on Mazandaron and killed all the relations of Mohammed Khan, who were ruling there, and took captive Agha Mohammed Khan, a boy only six years old, making him a eunuch. This boy was of Kojor race. When he was in the harem of Lutf-Ali, he kept thinking how his cruel master murdered his father and all his relations. When he sat on the royal rugs, he would take his revenge by cutting them. When he was of full age, twenty or twenty-five years old, he ran away to his own country, Mazandaron, and joined himself to his relations. He frequently attacked Lutf-Ali, and defeated him in 1795. He was then able to establish his throne in the southern part of Mazandaron. This great eunuch king founded the dynasty which rules to-day, restored the kingdom as it was under Karim-Kurd and conquered Georgia and Kharason. But he was assassinated May 14, 1797. His nephew, Futteh-Ali-Shah (1797-1834) engaged in three wars with Russia and was defeated each time. As a result he lost his territory in Armenia, and a great part of Persia, namely, from the Caucassian mountains to the River Aras, which now fixed the boundary between Russia and Persia. Futteh-Ali in his last war with Russia in 1826 was entirely defeated. Beside losing some part of his territory he paid the sum of 1,800,000,000 roubles ($9,000,000) to Russia. The death of the Crown Prince, Abbos Mirza, in 1833 seemed to give the final blow to the declining fortune of Persia, as he was the only man who seriously attempted to raise his country from the state of abasement into which it had fallen. Futteh-Ali had seven sons. One of them, Johon-Suz-Mirza, lives to-day. Seven years ago he was governor in the author's city; and came to visit the College of Oroomiah accompanied by a hundred princes and counts. He is a very ostentatious

FOUNDER OF THE PRESENT DYNASTY.

man. After the death of the Crown Prince each of the seven sons claimed to be inheritor of the throne while the father was still living. At the same time the Crown Prince, Abbos Mirza, had a son named Mohammed. Futteh-Ali, when quite old and near to death, by the aid of Russia made Mohammed, his grandson, king (1834-1848). Nayib-Al-Saltana acted as regent during the boyhood of Mohammed. When he came to power for himself he conceived the idea of restoring Bloogiston, Afghaniston and a great part of Turkoman to Persian dominion. He was especially anxious to take Herat, the key to India, but was resisted by England. The war was terminated in 1838.

Nasiruddin (defender of his religion), the late Shah, who was assassinated May 1, 1896, a young man eighteen years old, and very energetic, succeeded to the throne of his father in 1848. Following his father's example, the new Shah tried to restore Afghaniston and Bloogiston, but was compelled by England to sign an agreement on January 25, 1858, by which he was bound not to interfere further in the internal affairs of Herat.

In 1856 he violated this treaty and took the City of Herat. After a severe war with England in 1857, in which his loss was 20,000 soldiers, he relinquished Herat, but he added to

Persia many provinces in the western part of Afghaniston and Bloogiston, and also some states in Turkoman. He was one of the best kings of Persia. He visited Europe three times, once in 1873. He had European ideas, and was a well-educated man. He started a good system of postal telegraph, and had trained after the European discipline 30,000 soldiers. Above all, he founded a beautiful college in Teheran, which is called in Persian Daralfnoon (or the place of science). The present Shah, Mozuffur-uddin was born March 25, 1853, and succeeded to the throne of his father May 1, 1896. In 1892 the author saw him at Oroomiah College. He came with a large retinue to visit, being entertained at the home of Dr. Cochran. The work of the college pleased him, and he made it a gift of thirty pounds. He is a very kind and liberal man, especially toward the poorer of his subjects. We believe God will make him to be good to the oppressed Christians.

The list of kings who have reigned over Persia as regular kings make a total of 255.

CHAPTER III.

ARCHITECTURE OF PERSIA.

THE architecture of Persia is of considerable interest from the fact that the Persians added to their own the architecture of Assyria and Egypt, when they conquered those mighty empires. Hence the composite nature of the designs of some of her most famous buildings. A brief study of the old City of Persepolis will enable us the better to understand the nature of the architecture of this land, so rich in magnificent ruins. (The author wishes to give credit to McClintock and Strong's Encyclopedia for a large part of the following pages. He has extracted many quotations from this work.) This city, called "The Glory of the East," the ancient capital of Persia, is situated in the Province of Faris, on the River Araxes. Darius, Hastaspes, Xerxes, Artaxerxes and others tried to make it one of the grandest cities in all the world. Unfortunately it was destroyed by Alexander the Great, and now contains only some ruins of the royal palaces. First is the Chehly Minor *(forty pillars)*; also called Tokhtie-Jamshid, or throne of Jamshid. Some suppose that Jamshid was the founder of the city. Next in order is Nakhshie-Rustum, to the northwest. Near each of these palaces are the mounds of the tombs. The east building is the Harem of Jamshid, situated on a vast terrace of Cyclopean masonry, at the foot of a lofty mountain range. By far the most important is the first group, situated at the foot of a lofty mountain range. The extent of this terrace is about 1,500 feet from north to south and 800 feet from east to west, and was once surrounded by triple walls 16, 32 and 60 feet in height, respectively. The internal area is further divided into three terraces, the lowest one to the south; the central being about 800 feet square and rising 45 feet above the plain; and the third, the northern, about 550 feet long and 35 feet high. On the northern is the "Propyleum of Xerxes," but most distinguished here is the "Great Hall," of Xerxes, called Chehly Minor by way of eminence. The palace of Xerxes and that of Darius, towering one above the other in successive elevation, are also on this terrace. The stones used for this building are of dark gray marble, cut into gigantic square blocks, and in many cases exquisitely polished. The ascent from the plain to the great platform is made by two flights, the steps being nearly 22 feet wide, 3 1-2 inches high and 15 inches in tread, so that travellers have been able to ascend on horseback. The Propyleum of Xerxes is composed of two masses of stone work, which probably formed an entrance for foot passengers. The steps are paved with gigantic slabs of polished marble. The portal is still standing, and bears figures of animals 15 feet high. The building itself is conjectured to have been a hall 82 feet square, closely resembling the Assyrian halls of Nineveh. It bears the following inscription: "The great God Ahroomazda, He it is who has given this world, and who has given life to mankind, who has made Xerxes both king and lawgiver of the people. I am Xerxes the King and Great King, the King of Kings, the King of the many-peopled countries, the supporter of the great world, the son of King Darius, the Achoemenian."

"Says Xerxes the King, by the grace of Ahroomazda I have made this gate of entrance. There is many another nobler work besides this—Persepolis, which I have made, and which my father has executed."

An expanse of 162 feet divides this platform from the centre one, which bears many of those columns of the Hall of Xerxes, from which the ruins have taken their names. The stairs leading up to the Chehly Minor are still magnificent, according to the statement of Prof. Jooseph, whose residence was near this historic palace. The walls are superbly decorated with sculptures, representing colossal warriors with spears, gigantic bulls, combats with wild beasts, processions and the like, while broken capitals, shafts, pillars and countless fragments of buildings with cuneiform inscriptions cover the whole extent of the platform, 350 feet from north to south and 380 feet from east to west. The great Hall of Xerxes, perhaps the largest and most magnificent structure the world has ever seen, is computed to have been a rectangle of about 300 to 350 feet, and to have consequently covered two and a half acres. The pillars were arranged in four divisions, consisting of a central group, six deep every way, and an advanced body of twelve in two ranks, the number flanking the center. Fifteen columns are all that now remain of the number. Their form is very beautiful. Their height is 60 feet; the circumference of the shaft, 16 feet; the length from the capital to the turrets, 45 feet. Next along the west front stood the palace of Darius, and to the south the palace of Xerxes, measuring about 86 feet square, similarly decorated with lions, birds, heroes, kings and warriors.

Of course the present architecture of Persia is not equal to the old, for the evident reason that the country is not so rich as it was. However, the work in some cities is equivalent to ancient buildings. In modern times some splendid palaces have been erected of brick, either of raw or hardened by fire. These tower to a considerable height. The custom of Persia is to beautify without rather than within, so the exterior is painted with different colors. Blue, red and green are favorites. The walls are adorned with the pictures of flowers, birds, lions and many verses of Al-Kuran. Favorite poems also appear. Inside it is more plain, whitened by chalks. But the roof is wonderfully decorated with delicate chalk work. Here are sculptured designs of ladies holding bouquets of flowers, playing with doves on their shoulders and surrounded by beautiful objects. Usually in the center is a large mirror. This is all hand work. A single mason may work a month in completing the roof decorations of one room. All buildings are square. Village architecture is very poor. Buildings are one story in height, especially of Mohammedans. Most all are built of unburnt bricks. A Mohammedan peasant does not know the joy and pleasure of living. Though he has plenty of money, he is content to live in a small cottage, spending little.

Christians, on the other hand, are the direct reverse, and are learning to enjoy having things nice.

CHAPTER IV.

THE LANGUAGE AND POETRY OF PERSIA.

THE ancient languages of Persia are three: (1) The Zend or East Iranian, or Bactorian language. But this became obsolete during the third century before Christ. This was called the Zoroastrian language, because the name Zend is that of their sacred book. (2) The ancient Persian language, the chief remnants of which are found in the cuneiform inscriptions of the time of Archemides, discovered in the ruins of Persepolis on the rocks of Behiston. The inscriptions contain the names of gods, men and of Daniel the prophet. (3) The third language was Pehlawee, spoken by the West Iranians, Medians and Persians during the period of the Sassanidae—3rd to 7th century, A.D.

At last a new form of commentaries to the sacred writings came into existence, in which clearer and more distinct characters were used. Almost all old words of the Zend were replaced. This new form is called Pazend. In later times historians and the Arabs have called it Parsee.

It was in use from 700 to 1100 A.D. At 1100 the old Persian language was revived. This is called Jamie or Nizamic.

A purer dialect came into use as the direct result of the writings of the poet Hafiz, 1100 A.D., and has continued down to the present day. This is spoken especially in Shiraz, a city of great note in the history of Persia, and the capital of the state of Faris, which gives Persia its name.

Unfortunately after the Mohammedan conquest Persia fell under their reign. Arabs tried to infuse Arabic into the Persian language. The Koran was the only Holy Bible to them; they believed that its teachings should be accepted by all Parsees. All writers in the country now, as a matter of course, became Mohammedans. With the fanaticism characteristic of a conquering religion, with the ruthlessness which Islam has always shown, all the representatives of the old Persian literature and science were grievously persecuted by Omar's general, Sayid Ibn Abou Wakkas. All priests and writers were compelled to accept the new order of things: "Allah the only God, and Mohammed His prophet." So the pure language of the Parsees was infused with Arabic words to such an extent that one-third of the words of the language are Arabic.

POETICAL LITERATURE.

Under the dynasty of Samanides, a writer comes into view, one Nasr, living about 952 A.D., under the third ruler of the dynasty. Also Abul Hasson Rudige, the blind, lived under the same ruler. This man wrote 1,300-000 rhymes. About 1000 A.D., Kabbas wrote, being a contemporary of Mahmud who surrounded himself with four hundred court poets. Ansaric, another writer, wrote 300,000 rhymes in honor of the king.

The reign of Atabek dynasty was the brilliant age of Persian poetry. Auhaduddin Anawaree was one of the greatest writers of that period. The best mystic poet was Sunayi, author of 30,000 distichs. Nizami, about the twelfth century, was the founder of the Romantic Epoch. The greater part of his Jami or collection of five romantic poems, are about Khosraw and Shirin, a king and his betrothed; Magenoon and Leila, a lover and his beloved.

Kizilarsalon, the king, offered for each one of his poems not less than fourteen estates. His tomb now at Gendsheh is visited by hundreds of pious pilgrims.

In the eastern part of Persia the theosophical mysticism was pre-eminently cultivated, especially in Azerbijon state. A great number of these mystics are in Oroomiah, my city. They speak in allegorical form in glowing songs of wine and love.

Again in this province we find Sunayee in the thirteenth century and Fariduddin Attar, born 1216. A still greater man in this peculiar field was Djalal Eddin Romi, born at Balkh, and who died 1266. He was the founder of a still existing and most popular order of darwishes. His poems on contemplative life have made him the oracle of oriental mysticism up to this day.

I will give one of his rhymes which will show the spirit of his mysticism: "Gar Kasi wasf ou Zman Posad, bidil oz binishon chiguyan baz, ashikon kushtagon mashookand, bar nayayad Z kooshtagon awaz." The thirteenth century was one of the most brilliant in the annals of Persian poetry. The greatest seer of the era was Sheikh Musli Eddin Sahdie of Shiraz, who died in the year 1291. He stands unrivaled as Persia's foremost didactic poet. His Boston and Guliston—"the fruit of the garden and roses"—are universally known and loved in Europe.

At the beginning of the fourteenth century we made several meritorious imitations of Sahdi in didactic poetry. But far above all these, as above all other Persian lyrical and erratic poets, shines Hafiz. The "Sugar Lip" is a book in which he sang of wine and love, nightingale and flowers, bee and roses. Below is given a quotation from one of his poems about the nightingale and the miller: "Ai morgh saher ashk zparwana beyamoz, Kan sukhtara jan shud wawaz nayamad." Translation: "Oh, thou, the bird of morning, you must learn love from the miller. It burned itself in the fire, but did not make any noise." Haji Mollah Kozim translated this rhyme as follows: "The morning bird is the nightingale—little smaller than the sparrow, but it has a very loud voice, as clear as a golden bell. All poets in Persia agree that it is a better singer than any other bird in Asia. Besides his singing he is the bird that has more love for his mate than any other bird in the world. They generally sing in the morning and the evening time. When the female is on her nest the male sits in the same tree, or very near, and sings for his mate. At times the male sits on the nest, and, his mate perched near by sings for him in a wonderfully sweet voice. The nightingale is a general favorite, and many popular songs have been written about this bird, and are sung by nearly every young man and young lady, boy and girl in Persia.

This author says of the miller that it loves light more than any other insect. From its love of light it throws itself into the fire, as everyone has seen in America of a summer evening about an electric lamp. Sahdi takes this example for himself to illustrate his love to God. He says the love of the miller is more than the love of the nightingale, because the nightingale shows its love by singing and making noise; but the miller, though it has a living body, makes no noise when it is burning in the fire. "So," says he, "ought to be my love to God."

The city of Shiraz from the beginning until this day has been the seat of religion and especially of poetry because these two eminent poets, Sahdi and Hafiz, were born, lived, wrote and died here. Their tombs are visited annually by thousands of pilgrims. They are dead but their influence still lives and it has much effect on Persia and especially on the inhabitants of the city of Shiraz. Many students are enrolled at the great cathedral mosque in the city, where some of the ablest professors of the country are instructors. Professor Yooseph, a graduate of this institution, told me that the air and the very dust of that city has in it the spirit of poetry. Even the small boys who sell grapes, apples, etc., in the streets sing some very charming poems about their fruits, though they themselves may never have learned to read.

THE SWEETNESS OF THE PERSIAN LANGUAGE FOR POETRY.

The Persians have one poem about the sweetness of their language for poetry, as follows:

"The original language was the language of Arabs. The Turkish language is hard. But the Persian language is honey-comb." In comparison with the other Asiatic languages many scholars think it is indeed honey-comb and the sweetest of Asiatic languages, if not also of European languages, for the expression of poetry.

PART II. RELIGIONS.

CHAPTER I.

PARSEE RELIGION.

THIS was the prevailing religion of Persia in ancient times. Zerdush was either the founder or a reformer of that religion. The general belief is that he was the founder, since the religion and its followers are called by his name. Some suppose that this religion and the religion of Hindoo were originally the same, and that they were divided by some political affair between the Iranians and the Aryans. The Hindoo branch took the name Brahminian. The doctrines changed somewhat after the separation, but the fundamental principles remained the same.

Different dates are given for the beginning of the Zerdush religion. Some authorities date its beginning at 1200 B.C., while others place it at 500 B.C. The latter is generally agreed upon. There are two prevailing ideas about his place of birth, both Babylonia and Oroomiah, Persia, being claimed as his native city. There are many good reasons for believing that Oroomiah was his birthplace. First, the original worshippers were Persians, and the religion was started in Persia. Second, all Oriental scholars and writers supposed that this was his native city. Third, in the district immediately surrounding Oroomiah the writer has seen more than thirty immense hills of ashes, the remaining monuments of the fire worshippers of this religion. Fire was their god and a continuous flame was kept burning through the centuries. Some of these mountains of ashes are so huge in size that it would take a man an entire day to walk around it, and as high as the Masonic Temple of Chicago, a twenty-story office building. Some of these hills are named as following: De-ga-la, Sheikh—Ta-pa, Gog-ta-pa, etc. Among these hills we find the "Tower of Silence," a large structure built of stone and containing the remains of kings and other notable men of ancient times.

BIBLE AND DOCTRINES.

The bible of the Parsees is called Avesta, which means the revelation. The language is Zend, from which the Persian language is derived. The founder of this religion taught as pure monotheism as was taught by Mohammed. Zerdush taught the existence of but one deity, who was called Maz-daw, or, as it is pronounced now in Persia, Hurmizd. To this god was attributed the creation of all good fortune, government, long life, honor, health, beauty, truth, joy and happiness. But later this doctrine of monotheism became dualism, *i.e.*, the supposition of two primal causes of the real and intellectual world, the Vahu Mano; the good mind or reality and Akem Mano or the naught mind or naught reality. Ah-ra-man, the god of darkness has created devils, he causes evil thoughts, evil deeds, wars, misfortune, sorrow, death, and hell. Zerdush taught there are two lives, one mental and the other physical. He believed in the immortality of the soul; that there are two abodes for the departed, heaven, the house of angels, and hell, the dwelling-place of the devil and his angels. Between the two there is a bridge of judgment over which only the followers of Zerdush will be able to cross safely. Before the general resurrection the Sosiosh, the son of Zerdush, will be spiritually begotten. He will come as a messenger from Ahuramazdoo and will foretell the time of the resurrection and judgment. The world at that time will be utterly steeped in wretchedness and darkness and sin; will then be renewed; death, the archfiend of creation, will be slain and life will be everlastingly holy; and righteousness will dwell in the renewed world. This Zoroastrian creed flourished until the time of Alexander the Great throughout ancient Ironiona including Cabuliston, Bakhria, Media and Persia, and then declined. But again under Ardashir, who has been called Bobegon, and who claimed to be the descendant of Zerdush, the religion of his ancestors was renewed, and the lost parts of the holy book, Avesta, were found and put together. He chose a magician the ablest of 40,000 magician priests, to translate the book into vernacular language, thus renewing the religion. Unfortunately the Avesta was utterly destroyed in A.D. 640 by the followers of Mohammed.

Now we have in Persia only 15,000 Zoroastrians. The Mohammedans called them gabrees, *i.e.*, ungodly. Most of them live in Kerman Yezd on the soil of their motherland. The men are good citizens, humble, honest and generous, especially to their own brethren, and are industrious, intelligent, handsome, clean in appearance and faithful to their religion. The women are most beautiful, delicate in frame, small hands, small nose, clear complexion, with pink cheeks, black eyes and eyebrows. They do not cover their faces when in public, except to Mohammedans, whom they consider wicked men. The women are good, faithful housewives and honest to their husbands.

THEIR RITUALS.

A Parsee child must be born on the ground floor of the house of its parents as a sign of humility and that the child may begin its life with good thoughts, words and actions, and as a sign of loyalty to its parents. The mother cannot go out for forty days. After that she washes herself with holy water which has been sanctified by the priest.

A Parsee rises early, washes his hands and face, and recites his prayers toward the sun. He rejects pork, ham and camel flesh and will not eat anything cooked by one outside of the Parsee religion. Marriages can be contracted only with persons of their own creed. Polygamy is forbidden except after nine years of sterility, then a man is allowed to marry another woman. Divorces are entirely forbidden. The crimes of fornication and adultery are very severely punished. They worship the clean creations of the great Hurmizda such as the sun, moon, fire, etc. Aha-ramazda is the origin of light, the sun and fire having come from him, he having first been created by Hurmizda. In the case of a hopelessly sick person the priest will recite some text of the holy bible Avesta, as a consolation to the dying person. After death the body is taken to the ground floor, the place of its birth, to be washed and anointed with perfumes, dressed in white and put upon an iron grating. A dog is brought in to take a last look, and he drives away all evil spirits. The friends and relatives go before the door, bow down and raise their hands to their heads after touching the floor, as an indication of their last respect to the departed soul. The body upon the bier is covered. Two men will bring it out and give it to four pall-bearers dressed in white, who, followed by a great procession, take it to the "Tower of Silence." The last prayer will be recited in the holy temple a building in which the holy fire burns continually through the ages. The body is then taken from the "Tower of Silence" and placed on an iron bier, is exposed to the fowls of the air and the dew of heaven and to the sun until the flesh has disappeared, and the bleached bones fall through into a pit beneath, and are afterwards buried in a cave.

They believe the holy fire is brought down from heaven. Only priests can approach it and they must wear a half-mask over the face lest their breath should defile it, and never touch it with hands, but by instruments. Tobacco smoking is prohibited, as the smoker would defile the holy fire. They say there are five kinds of fire and great respect is shown to them. I remember having had a conversation with a Parsee in which he said: "Fire purifies all things, is stronger than all things, is cleaner than all other things, more beautiful than all things; therefore, fire is *god*. Your own Bible says: 'I am a consuming fire.'"

The Parsees have five kinds of sacrifices. These are the slaughtering of animals for the public and poor men; prayer, the Doruns sacrament with its consecrated bread and wine in honor of the founder of the law, Heromah (or Sama) and Dahman. This sacrament resembles our Lord's Supper. It is eaten publicly as a feast of joy. Fourth, the sacrifice of expiation, which is offered by all men and is killed in their temples. Lastly, the sacrifice for the souls of the dead. The removal of moral and physical impurities is effected by holy water and earth and by prayer. Prayer and holy words from the Avesta are recited several times every day. Fasting and celibacy are hateful to the divinity. The ethical code may be summed up in three words—purity of thought, of words and of deeds. This, they claim, will become the universal religion of the world.

A Parsee believes the soul of a dead man is

for three days walking near the tomb where the dead body is laid. The fourth day the gates of heaven will be opened and he will approach the bridge of Chin-vat. Here the good and evil deeds of his life will be weighed in the balances of justice. If the good deeds of his life outweigh the bad, he will pass over the bridge into heaven. If the bad are heavier than the good the candidate falls beneath the bridge into hell. In both heaven and hell there are three states. In heaven, good words, thoughts and deeds; in hell, bad words, thoughts and deeds.

CHAPTER II.

MOHAMMEDANISM.

MOHAMMED means "Praised One." One of the Mohammedan divines once spoke in the presence of the writer of the similarity in the Arabic language of "Ahamad" and the "Holy Spirit," and he claimed to believe that Ahamad or Mohammed was the Holy Spirit which Jesus promised to send into the world. When told in reply that Jesus promised to send the Comforter into the world immediately after His departure, and that Mohammed did not live until 570 years after Christ, the priest had no more to say.

This great prophet of the desert who converted the wild Arabs was born about A.D. 570, at Mecca. He was the only child of Abdulla, and his mother, Halima, both from the noble family of Koreish, who claimed that they were the descendants of Ismael and that their family was hereditary guardians of the sacred Kaaba mosque, in which was kept the holy black stone worshipped by all Arabs.

The Moslems have many legends and traditions regarding the birth of Mohammed. The sun moved from its place and gave a more brilliant light, with the seven colors of the rainbow; the angels bowed themselves to him and sung a new song in heaven; all the trees were shaken as by a strong wind. He was born circumcised and with his navel cut. A seal of prophecy was written on his back in letters of light. Immediately prostrating himself on the ground he raised his hands and prayed. Three persons as brilliant as the sun, one holding a silver goblet, another an emerald tray, and the third a silken towel appeared in company with the angel Gabriel, the latter holding in his hand a knife. Gabriel cut open the child's belly, the first angel poured cleansing water over the child to wash away all sin, the second held the emerald tray beneath him, and the third dried him with the silken towel, and then all saluted him and called him the "prince and saviour of mankind." His father died at the age of twenty-five years, before his son was born. He left his widow five camels, a few goats, and a slave girl, her name being Amina. At the age of six years Mohammed had a fit of epilepsy. He frequently fell down and foamed at the mouth, and snored like a camel. About this time his mother died, and he was reared by his grandfather, Abdul-mota-Kalib, and his uncle, Abu-ta-lif, and nursed by his faithful slave, Amina. For a time he herded goats, a disreputable occupation among Arabs. But he afterwards glorified in it, pointing to the example of Moses and David and saying that God never called a prophet who had not before been a shepherd. In appearance he was of medium size, slender, but broad-shouldered, and of strong muscles, black eyes and hair, white teeth, oval-shaped face (which is now much praised among Mohammedans), a long nose, patriarchal beard, and a commanding look. His step was quick and firm. He wore common garments of white cotton stuff, and mended his own clothing and did everything possible for himself and aided his wives in household affairs. He had fourteen wives besides concubines. He possessed a vivid imagination and a genius for poetry and religious doctrines, but was not learned and perhaps could not read nor write.

He became servant for a very wealthy widow named Khadijah, and made several caravan journeys for her to Syria and Palestine with great success. Afterwards he won the heart of the widow and married her against the will of her father. He was twenty-five years of age and the widow was forty-five years old. Marriage proved happy and was fruitful with four daughters and two sons, but all died except one little daughter, Fa-ti-ma. Mohammed adopted Ali, his nephew, and married his daughter Fa-ti-ma to him. She became the mother of all the prophet's descendants. Mohammed loved his first wife, Kha-di-jah, was faithful to her, and after her death always cherished her memory, as she was the first person to believe in his doctrines.

On his journeys to Palestine and Syria he became acquainted with Jews and Christians and got an imperfect knowledge of their religion and traditions. At that time the Jews and Christians had scattered the ideas of monotheism among the Arabs. Some of the Arabs were tired of worshipping false idols and embraced the faith in one God. One of these men was Mohammed. He became zealous to establish a religion throughout Arabia, to teach and compel men to worship only one God and to recognize himself as His only prophet. He spent many days and nights in the caves of Mount Hira, near Mecca, in meditation and prayer. His zealous efforts to establish his faith brought a return of the violent convulsion and epileptic fits of earlier days, and his enemies said he was possessed with demons. He started preaching to the ignorant classes of Arabs, teaching them that there was only one living God who created heaven and earth and all mankind. In A.D. 610, his fortieth year, he claimed to have received a call from the angel Gabriel while in a trance in Mount Hira, directing him to say: "In the name of God." Many times after this first meeting he communicated with Gabriel in these caves and saw many visions. Once, when almost discouraged, he waited for further enlightenment in visions to qualify him for the duties of his office as prophet—if not to commit suicide—when suddenly Gabriel, at the end of the horizon appeared, saying: "I am Gabriel and thou art Mohammed the prophet of God, fear not." After this assurance, he commenced his career as a prophet and founder of a new religion. His doctrines were gathered from three religions, the Jewish, Christian and Arabic. He taught that there is only one Allah—Almighty God, ever-present and working will. Henceforth the revelations came from time to time, sometimes like the sound of a bell conversing with him; at other times Gabriel came down and spoke to him. For the first three years he worked among his family. Kadijah was his first believer. His father-in-law, Abu-Baker, Omar, a young, energetic man, his daughter Fatima, his son-in-law Ali and other faithful followers to the number of forty, were the first disciples of this new religion, and were very influential in spreading the same. Then he publicly announced that he had a command from God, and had been given the divine office as prophet and law-giver. As his notoriety spread, pilgrims flocked to Mecca, and he preached to them, attacking the idolatry of Mecca. When his enemies demanded a miracle from him, he responded by producing the Koran leaf by leaf as occasion demanded. He provoked persecution; and civil war followed. In A.D. 622 he was forced to flee for his life from Mecca to Medina, a distance of 250 miles. This flight is called Higira, meaning the flight (July 15, 622), from which the era of Islam begins.

In Medina he was generally accepted as a prophet of God. His method was at first toleration. He said: "Let there be no compulsion in religion," but afterwards said: "All infidels must accept one God and Mohammed his prophet. If men refuse, kill them, plunder their property, and their wives and daughters are for you." The wild Arabs were kindled by this command. His followers were all robbers except some of the leaders. In 624, with an army of 305, all citizens of Medina, he gained a victory over his strong enemy, Koreish, whose army was double the size of Mohammed's. By other engagements he rapidly conquered Jews and Christians. After one battle 600 Jews were massacred at his order and their wives and daughters were made slaves. In 627 he triumphantly entered Mecca, and in 630 he demolished 360 idols; then Koreish, a leading tribe, shouted, "There is but one God and Mohammed is His prophet." Ten years after Higira, with 40,000 Moslems he made his last journey to Mecca, and subdued all Arabia. Upon returning to Medina, he died in his home and in the arms of Ayesha, his favorite wife, June 8th, 632, at the age of sixty-three years.

When on his deathbed and suffering extreme pain and anguish his friends expressed surprise that a great prophet should suffer so. He called their attention to the fact that one prophet of olden times was eaten by worms, while another was so poor as to have only a rag to cover his shame, and stated that a prophet is not rewarded here, but hereafter. His last words were a prayer for the destruction of all Jews and Christians because they were so hard to convert. He prayed: "O Lord, let not my tomb be an object of worship. Let there remain only one faith, that of Islam, in all Arabia. Gabriel come near me; Lord pardon me, grant me joy, accept me into Thy companionship on high," etc.

Mohammed did not claim the power of performing miracles, but since his death some of his followers have attributed miracles to him, such as, when walking the streets, trees and stones would salute him; he caused a flood of water to spring up from dry ground; he rode on his horse Borak through air from Medina to Mecca, Jerusalem to paradise and to the heavenly mansions, and again came back to Mecca. The only miracle Mohammed himself claimed was the revelation of Koran.

HIS CHARACTER.

Some people have the impression that Mohammed was a man of good character and great simplicity. Possibly this was true of him in the earlier part of his life, but he degenerated as Solomon; but, unlike the wise preacher of "vanity," he never repented. Mohammed was a slave of sensual passion. The doctrine of polygamy which he taught was the result of his own sensuality. Ayesha, his favorite wife, said: "The prophet loves three things—women, perfumes and food." He, at the age of fifty-three years, married this woman when she was at the age of nine years. Again he claimed to have a special revelation from heaven to marry Zey-nab, the wife of his adopted son. To gratify this wish, it was necessary for Zeyd, his faithful son, to get a divorce from Zey-nab.

THE CONQUEST OF ISLAM.

"The secret of success for Islam is in the sword," said Mohammed. His faith teaches that one drop of blood shed for Allah, or God, avails more than all prayer, fastings and sacrifices. One night spent in the holy armies of Islam will be rewarded by Allah more than human reason can think. Everyone that falls in battle is received in heaven as a martyr and rewarded for his devotion to the faith. After Mohammed's death, his successor became aggressive as his forces grew stronger. His command to his armies was: "Before you is paradise, behind you is hell." Inspired by this belief, the wild and superstitious Arabs rushed forward and subdued Syria, Palestine and Egypt. The churches in the large cities of these lands were converted into mosques for the worship of Mohammed.

In 668 and 717 they besieged Constantinople, and in 707 subdued the northern provinces of Africa. In 711 they established a Califat in Spain at Cordova. The Arabs crossed the Pyrenees and made the threat that they would soon stable their horses in St. Paul's Cathedral at Rome. But they were defeated by Charles Martel in 732. Ferdinand drove them out of Spain into Africa. In the East the Moslems had in the ninth century subdued Persia, Afghaniston, Bloogiston, a large part of India, also a large part of Brahmanism and Buddhism. The Turks were conquered in the eleventh century; the Mongols in the thirteenth century. Constantinople fell into the hands of the unspeakable Turks in 1453. The magnificent church of St. Sophia, in which Chrysostom preached the Gospel with a fiery tongue, and many church fathers chanted in it the true Word of God, was converted into a mosque. To-day the Koran is read there instead of the Gospel. The Sultan occupies the throne of Constantine and calls himself the "shadow of the Almighty," boasts in his fanatical religion, and scorns Christian powers. On the other hand, the Christian powers look at him with the cold spirit of Christianity, but I believe the time will come and is near when the Gospel will be preached again in the Church of St. Sophia instead of the Koran.

CHAPTER III.

THE MOHAMMEDAN RELIGION.

THE Koran is the Mohammedan's holy bible, creed and code of laws. The holy Koran was delivered to Mohammed neither in graven tablets of stone nor by cloven tongues of fire, but it was engraven on Mohammed's heart and was communicated by his tongue to the Arabs. His heart was the Sinai where he received his revelation, and his tablets of stone were the hearts of believers. The Koran contains 114 chapters and 6,225 verses. Each chapter begins with the formula, "In the name of God the merciful and the compassionate." The chapter is named from the chief subject treated therein; as "praise," "the light," "the spider," "the woman," etc. Mohammed received all of his revelation at once, but when occasion required he dictated new chapters to Zeid. Another notion is that the Koran was delivered orally and was scattered until after the prophet's death, when it was collected by Ayesha, his youngest wife, and Zeid. All of it was written in the best classical poetry. It is sweet in the Arabic language, but it looses its beauty when translated into other languages.

Mohammed did not invent a new religion, but collected most of his doctrines from the Jewish, heathen and Christian religions and Christian tradition. Mohammed was greatly indebted to a Nestorian monk named Sargius Be-hi-ra, a man of rare ability, whom the prophet kept in his home for several years and learned all he knew about Christian doctrines and traditions. Many of the wise counsels, stories, teachings of our duties to God and brethren in the faith, that are related in the Old and New Testaments are reproduced in the Koran, but the language is changed and the order of their occurrence is reversed. The Koran contains mistakes, such as making the Virgin Mary the mother of our Lord the same person as Mary the sister of Moses and Aaron. But, without question, the Koran is one of the greatest books of the world in the number of adherents it has. It is a code of civil and religious law; 200,000,000 Mohammedans scattered all over the world to-day are following the teaching of the Koran. The book contains much that is good and wise, but one of its most dangerous defects is the prominence and approval given to polygamy and sensualism.

CHAPTER IV.

THE CREED OF ISLAM.

MONOTHEISM is the corner-stone of Islam. Their creed consists of six articles—God, predestination, the angels good and bad, the books and traditions of the 124,000 prophets, the resurrection and judgment, eternal reward and punishment. The formula continually repeated by the Mohammedans is this: "There is no god but God and Mohammed is His prophet." Allah, or God, has infinite power and wisdom and is holy, omnipotent, omnipresent, creator of the universe, upholder of all. He is an arbitrary ruler, but deals justly with men. He is an object of fear and reverence, rather than of love and gratitude. The Mohammedan does not look upon God as the Father. He says God is the Almighty Creator, and men ought to fear and tremble before Him as slaves. The writer was reasoning with a Mohammedan one day and spoke of God as "our Heavenly Father." He said, "You blaspheme; don't call God a father. This could not be, as he never had a wife. Allah has foreordained all things, good and evil. An unconditional resignation to Him is true wisdom. He is known because He has revealed

Himself through chosen messengers, angelic and human, such as Adam, Noah, Abraham, Moses, and Jesus, our great and chief prophets, but Mohammed is the last and the greatest above all."

CHAPTER V.

THE PRIESTHOOD.

THE Muj-ta-hid is the highest order of the priesthood, but this order is divided into four degrees. The members of the highest degree reside at Karballa, the sacred city. The chief of this degree is called Naib-el-emam and, in the belief of Shiites Moslems, he is the representative of Mohammed. His position is the same as that of the Pope in the Roman Catholic Church; and he is believed to be infallible. His authority extends over the entire clergy and in some respects over government. He resides in the most holy mosque, which was built on the tombs of Hassan and Hussein, children of Ali, who were martyrs in the war between Shiites and Sun-neh Moslems. He has power to declare holy war. Vast sums of money are contributed into his keeping every year, which he spends in defraying the expenses of thousands of pilgrims who flock to this shrine, and also for students who study in that mosque. He leads a simple life, but it was stated by one of the pilgrims that he makes considerable money for his children. When this great chief dies there is a day of lamentation throughout Persia, and lords and counts feed thousands of poor men and divide money among them. All business is suspended for the day.

The late Shah, it is said, sent three different messengers to this high Church official before he could get an interview, the churchman pleading humility and unworthiness to receive the king, but before the latter departed after the interview he was charged to be a good and faithful ruler.

The second degree in the Muj-ta-hid is called Arch-muj-ta-hid. It is composed of four priests who reside in the four places known as Era-wanee, Shirazee, Khorasonee and Isphahonee, and one of these officials succeeds Naib-el-emam at the death of the latter.

The third degree is the common Muj-ta-hid, who are numerous. In my city (Oroomiah) of 30,000 inhabitants there are ten or more priests of this degree. Sometimes they are called Eulama, meaning divines.

THE METHOD OF THEIR LIVING.

They are executors of civil and religious law; no man can be a judge or lawyer unless he is a

Muj-ta-hid. These priests judge such cases as the division of property, for which they charge a fee. Where the interested parties are rich they are frequently required to appear before the priest several times before a decision is given that he may charge them a larger fee. As a general rule, the man who pays these priest-magistrates the most money will win the case, even if it is necessary to pervert the law. Many a well-to-do man has been brought to poverty by the extortions of these Muj-ta-hid. Government cannot resist them. When lords or counts or rich people marry, they charge large sums of money for performing the ceremony. Large fees are also made for writing legal documents in the transference of land or other valuable property. The common people consider it a privilege to make presents to the Muj-ta-hid. These men are usually very rich, and own one or more beautiful palaces and have from two to four wives. Every young widow who has beauty and riches is sought in marriage by some of the priests.

The fourth degree is called Mollah, and their office is the same as the Protestant elder. The Mohammedans have no preaching services such as we have, except on holidays, when certain ceremonies are carried out. The Mollah visit the sick, call on families, teach them prayers and traditions and conduct funerals. Some of them teach children, who come to them each day for instruction. Their meals are provided by the students, who bring them some food, usually very choice, each morning. One dime a month is generally the tuition fee. In the fall his parishioners who are able give him a collection of provisions for the winter, such as grapes, apples, wheat, fuel, etc. He is highly respected in the community, and is always invited out to a feast in some private home on holidays. He writes documents for the people, for which he gets from two to ten cents, but the fee is often two or three eggs or a basket of fruit. This is the poor Mollah's only income. Some of them have no parish and do secular work for a living, others recite Koran on the tomb of a lord, for which they are paid by the relatives of the deceased. I have seen one Mollah reciting Koran for fifteen years at the tomb of a noted army officer.

There are a class of priests, more learned and devout, who work as the revivalists of their religion. On holidays, which are quite frequent, the mosques are crowded with worshippers, when one of these priests mounts an elevated pulpit with great ostentation and in an impressive voice begins to read or repeat Koran He will chant traditions of the prophets and martyrs and relate pathetic stories of the noble sacrifices of departed heroes of the faith. His charming tones and utterances have much effect on his audience, and men and women weep and beat their breasts.

THE GARMENTS OF THE MUJ-TA-HID.

The Muj-ta-hid wears underclothes of white linen; his long coat is made of woolen cloth. His outer cloak is a robe that hangs to the feet. This robe is quite expensive, being made of the fur of animals, and is dyed yellow. They believe it a duty to wear a robe of skin as a sign of meekness. The robes cost from $50 to $500. He wears a girdle of white linen in many folds. His turban is large and white. The light, heelless shoes cover only half of his feet. When he goes out he has a fine staff in his hand, the handle being of gold or silver. From ten to twenty servants accompany him, some stepping before, others after him. Men of all classes rise and salute him by bowing with their hands across their breast. Many men kiss the shoes of the high Muj-ta-hids.

THE PLACE OF SAY-YIDS IN MOHAMMEDANISM.

Mohammedanism is divided into two great sects, viz., Shiites and Sunnites. Both hold Mohammed to be the prophet and Saviour of mankind and Koran to be the holy bible, written by the finger of God and given to Mohammed through the mediation of Gabriel. But they differ in their belief as to who are the true successors of Mohammed. Shiites claim that Ali the son-in-law and nephew of Mohammed was Caliph, while Sunnites contend that four disciples of Mohammed were his true successors. This difference led to war and bloodshed and gave rise to a permanent division in Mohammedanism.

Persia generally belongs to the Shiites tribe. They receive Ali as the Caliph after Mohammed. The descendants of Ali are therefore held in high esteem and rank in Persia. They are called Say-yids, which means prophets and masters, and they have privileges that do not belong to common men. They are very zealous to perpetuate their own sect. From the time of Ali they have kept a careful record of their genealogy. This book of testimony, called Sajjara, is given from father to son and serves as a credential to the Say-yidical tribe. Each family must have in its possession a credential at least two hundred years old. When these are worn by age and use their leaders may draft copies and duly certify them.

The Say-yid's dress distinguishes him from other men. He wears a green turban and girdle, so that he is really known whether alone or in a throng. If a common man should presume to wear these articles of dress, he would be severely punished. The Say-yid's turban is to him more precious than a kingly crown. It is the sign of their glory. The girdle is a symbol of strength. Their rank is higher than all other degrees among men, and their high priest is more honored than a prince. So Say-yid ruleth over other men. He demands and receives their honors. In the assemblies of lords and influential men the Say-yid occupies the chief seats, and are always served first. Oaths of gravity are sworn by their heads. All men fear them, believing that their curse will surely be brought to pass. They are never smitten or reviled. If a Christian should lift his hand against them that hand must be severed from his body. They are exempt from legal punishment. Governors cannot impose on them fines or imprisonments. If a Say-yid should kill a common man it would be impossible to punish him with death for the murder. The governor cannot punish him, for it would be a sin against God; it is believed that God created all men for the sake of Mohammed and his descendants. A Say-yid's punishment must come through the leader of that order.

Many vows are made to them. Parents, when their daughters are sick, vow to marry them to a Say-yid, believing that God will cure them for the sake of the Say-yid. They generally ride on gray horses, claiming that those of that color belong to them. They lead the large pilgrim caravans, which go every year to worship at the tomb of Ali. Their presence is believed to protect the caravans from thieves and robbers. Their law gives them authority over the property of other men. They are masters while others are peasants. Sometimes they smite and punish other men without mercy. By their law one-tenth of all property belongs to them. Generally, they do not work, but live well, because of their position as Say-yids, or holy men. The more noble of them will sit in their houses and receive tithes of the fruits, coffee, tea and money of the surrounding people. If these tithes are not freely given, a servant will be sent with authority to demand and take same. The less noble of the Say-yids go personally to the homes, vineyards and gardens and gather their portion. Sometimes there might be seen no less than ten Say-yids going to vinyards for this purpose. Generally they ask nothing from Christians, as their law restrains them, and they are ashamed to ask of other religions.

I once met a Say-yid in my father's vineyard and he asked a portion. I refused, telling him that I myself was also a Say-yid, *i.e.*, a Christian Say-yid, and asked if one Say-yid should receive something from another. He laughed and said:

HIGH CLASS DERVISH.

"Yes, sir, sometimes." I gave him three pounds of raisins. These Say-yids are in only the Shiites branch of Islam. In later years their honor has decreased; the government is against them. Some of them are very religious. Two of them in the city of Ispha-han were converted to Christianity and suffered martyrdom. One has been converted to Christianity in my city, Oroomiah. He is one of the most spiritual men among Christians.

THE DARWISHES.

Shiites Mohammedanism rests upon two pillars, one of which is Darwishes. This is one of the most holy orders of the Musalmans. It corresponds to the monasticism of Christianity. It contains several degrees, such as asceticism, mandicanism, etc. It is a volunteer consecration to Ali and his prophet, except in cases in which parents had dedicated their sons to the order. There are numerous instances in which women without children made a vow to Allah that if given a son they would consecrate him to God to be a Darwish. This order contains members from all classes, high and low, rich and poor, and even from the royal family. Celibacy is not required, but they are taught that it is far better for them not to marry.

THEIR CHARACTER.

A Darwish is expected to be, and usually is, humble, kind and liberal, ready to serve any man. He must suffer all the trouble of life and live in an humble condition because this is holiness. He is required to be well informed in all religious stories, tradition and Koran, and particularly in the poetical writings of Maw-le-wee order, which is their own order, founded by Anwa-ree, the father of the Darwishes. Some of the members know from one to five thousand of these sacred poems. Most of them are sufficiently educated to read. The Darwishes are the most faithful, honest and pure of all the followers of Mohammed. In all my life I have never heard of a single immoral Darwish. Some of them are very intelligent and well educated, and familiar with all their religious rites. On the other hand, they are very superstitious, fanatical and ambitious to propagate their religion, believing it to be a true religion. They are free to discuss their faith with all men in a kind spirit. In a discussion with one of them he could not answer me, but proposed that we prove the truth of our religion by both entering a burning fire, and the one who came out unharmed would have the true religion. I told him to enter the fire and if he was not burned I would believe in his religion and become a Mohammedan. He did not dare do it, and was ashamed.

THE NATURE OF THEIR SERVICE.

The darwishes' work is to tell stories, tales and traditions during week days in the streets. Friday is holy day among Mahommedans and is to be observed in worshipping God. The darwishes begin at one o'clock p.m. on that day singing poems on the streets and continue until evening.. Their poems are for the glory and honor of Mohammed and Ali, for they believe these two men were the supreme creation of God. One of their poems reads as follows :

" The first of creatures is Ali ; the supreme of beings is Ali ; the true calif of the prophet all is Ali; the lord of all the world is Ali; the lord of my soul is Ali."

The darwish wears long hair, and a pointed orange-shape cap, a cloak of patchwork and a long white robe, and in his right hand a tomahawk with a fancy handle with some poems written on the blade. In the other hand is held a kashkul for the collection of money. These are the rituals of his office. A dozen or more of them may be seen on every street, not far from each other, standing in front of the stores singing some poems for the praise of Ali in a loud voice, and with an earnest and enthusiastic spirit. Then he will pass his kashkul and the shopman will drop in it from one to three pennies and sometimes only a bit of sugar or ginger. Any gift is acceptable. One passing in the streets hears voices of base, tenor, etc., some rough, some clear as the sound of a bell of gold making an attractive melody. Sometimes they sing two by two, one for the praise of Mohammed, the other for the praise of Ali. Once I heard a darwish singing a poem to the praise of Ali, and when he had finished another responded near by singing to the praise of Mohammed in the following words: "He (Mohammed) has attained to the supremacy of his personal holiness; he has enlightened the darkness by personal beauty; beautiful are all his deeds. The blessings of God be upon him and upon all his children." Some darwishes travel over all Persia, spending a short time in each city they visit doing their work.

The cap which the darwish wears has embroidered upon it a verse from Koran and signifies his consecration to the service of Allah. The kashkul is a box in which to collect money for the poor and sick. The white robe is a sign of purity. The sheepskin on his shoulder is a sign of meekness. The beads on his neck are to remind him of the duty of prayer. The tomahawk is a sign of war and victory for his prophet and Allah. Those who have excelled in their holy service go to their leader and he places on the skin of the right shoulder of the darwish an inscription which remains as a sign of consecration and honor.

There is a low class of darwishes who are very ignorant, superstitious and fanatical and are like beggars. They pitch their tents at the gates of rich people and will not go away until they have been satisfied with money. Sometimes a large crowd of this class will gather in a mosque and spent several hours in howling unto Allah and the prophets until made weary by the exertion.

When the good darwish goes home Friday evening, he will have gathered some money and also provisions, such as tea, coffee, sugar, etc. He will keep for himself and family enough to last one week; the remainder is given to the poor.

THEIR PLACE IN MOHAMMEDAN RELIGION.

The darwish is highly respected by all classes from the royal family to the most humble. No man dares to beat or lay hands on one of them, as it would be considered a great crime. In case a darwish does wrong or commits crime, the government does not punish him, but refers the matter to the leader of the order. Sometimes they are called Kallander, which means humble and holy men of Allah. They are exempted from paying taxes and from military service. Many presents are given to them by the people. The salutation is different from the common people. The first says, "Ya-ho" which means: "O living God"; the response is "Ya-mal-ho," which means : "O God the giver of life."

So it is plain that the darwishes are one of the two pillars that support Islamism. Thank God we have some darwishes converted to Christianity.

❧

CHAPTER VI.

THE LAYMEN.

THE laymen are divided into three classes, viz., the counts or lords, middle class and low class.

The middle class live mostly in towns and cities. Their occupation is merchandise ; to carry goods to Europe and import goods into Persia. Others are manufacturing carpets, rugs, etc. Others are ironsmiths, silversmiths, carpenters, druggists, butchers and masons. A great number are secretaries for lords, counts, and in military service. The life of this class is very happy indeed. Their homes are quite comfortable, and kept in good order. Their tables are spread with enough of the good things to satisfy. This class do none of the work that custom has assigned to the lower classes. Pride would not allow it. Custom requires them to have smooth hands—not always white, for some prefer to dye them red.

The women of the middle class take life easy. They are not often allowed to go outside without permission of their husbands or mothers-in-law. In some instances the older ladies spend their time making rugs, shawls, and carpets—some of which are very beautiful and costly. The young ladies and brides spend their time in making caps, purses, head-covering, dresses, etc. An unmarried girl is positively required and it is the duty of her mother to teach her how to make rugs, carpets and embroidery work, etc., for her marriage. One of her first duties is to learn to dress herself handsomely. The face and brow will be colored with red and white paints. The eyes and eyebrows with black paint. The hands and feet are dyed with hana, a kind of paint that colours them red.

COSTUMES AT HOME.

The shirt worn at home by women is an article made of silk or cotton. It is short, open-breasted, well embroidered, is red or white and reaches to the middle of the thigh. Over the shirt is the cula-ja, rather loose, with long sleeves fastened with buttons of silver.

The shalwar is similar to the ordinary skirt, only it is very short. Some wear from three to ten of these skirts. The outer one is very rich and trimmed with gold lace. The head covering is called char-kat and is made square of a long, embroidered article of fine silk or thin cotton, and is fastened under her chin. Sometimes at home they are bareheaded. Hose are white and long. The hair is generally black, heavy, braided and spread on her back. In front it is parted in the middle when bangs are not worn. The hair is usually painted to appear black and smooth.

HER JEWELRY

The middle class of women are fond of jewelry, but do not burden themselves with heavy ornaments as do some of the lower class. They usually wear two or three finger rings, small ear-rings of gold, bracelets and necklace. There is frequently a large emerald, incased in gold,

HAREM COSTUME.

hanging from the necklace, bearing this inscription: "There is no god but Allah." Beautiful ornaments of gold and silver are attached to the ends of their braided hair.

When a wife has perfumed and adorned herself, she will await the coming of her husband from his shop. She knows at what time he will return home. An hour before his coming she will go before the mirror to see if she is dressed beautifully enough to please her husband. Ten minutes before his arrival she will prepare a delicious kalyon (which is a smoke and water pipe). Holding it in her hand she will rise and offer him the kalyon, saying, "My lord, command your pleasure." He will take the pipe and smoke. While he is sitting she will sprinkle perfume on his head and clothes. For several minutes they exchange the pipe and smoke alternately. This is the first thing which a husband of the middle class expects of his wife—not to work for him but to adorn herself and please him. It cannot be said that the Mohammedan does not love his wife. He buys her whatever she asks for; not because he considers her his equal, but for the sake of his own pleasure.

MEN'S COSTUME.

Most men of the middle class, at some time in life, go on a pilgrimage to Mecca and Medina.

After a pilgrim returns he is given the title of Ha-jeh and thereafter wears a turban on his head instead of the ordinary cap. The cap commonly worn by the Persian is about eight inches high, has no brim and is black in color. The shirt is of white cotton, open in front and fastened with a button on the right shoulder. The trousers are very much like the bloomers worn by some bicyclists of modern times, and old people wear garments even wider than bloomers. They are made of wool or cotton and are usually black. The coat is called ar-ka-look. Some are long enough to reach the ankle, while others reach about the middle of the thigh. The sleeves fasten at the wrist by a button of silk cord. There is a pocket on either side near the belt. Various colors are worn. The gima or overcoat is a heavy wool garment reaching to the knee, the lower part of which is pleated. It is opened in front and fastened with a number of buttons. The belt is a large piece of linen folded many times around the waist. Some wear heavy and costly shawls.

It is a general custom to shave the head except a small place on each side of the head just over the ear and a spot on the crown of the head. The hair-covered spots are called zoolf and are dyed with hana. The most religious men and the aged shave the entire surface of the head. The young men shave the beard, except the mustache, till the age of thirty years, after which time the beard is clipped at the length of about one inch till the age of forty. After the age of forty the beard is never cut. The mustache is never shaved by young or old. It is a mean thing to do, and is against their religion. No man has been seen in Persia with a smooth upper lip except Europeans. A man who will shave his mustache is not a Mohammedan but an infidel; not a man, but a girl. The long mustache is regarded as the glory of man.

THE LOWER CLASS.

The lower class of people are farmers and day laborers and among them is much misery. They work long hours and get from fifteen to twenty-five cents a day. Their clothing is of cheap material, poorly made, and shorter than the garments of the higher classes. In order to save time and soap their clothes are sometimes not washed for a month. Some farmer's wives use the sickle all day long in the field during harvest-time. Many women do the lighter work of killing weeds. Sometimes a woman will take her babe to the field with her and leave it in the care of an older child while she labors. In the fall of the year the laborers are busy in the vineyards, a great abundance of grapes being produced in this country. A familiar scene of an evening is to see men and women trudging homeward bearing heavy burdens of fruit, raisins, etc., stored in baskets. Some of the children are employed through the day looking after and feeding the cattle, buffaloes and sheep, while it is the duty of others to carry food and drink to the workers in the fields. In the winter the men are employed feeding cattle or in weaving coarse cloths for the clothing of the lower class. Others who are not thus engaged spend the winter in carrying dried fruits, wheat, fuel and various kinds of goods to the cities on donkey caravans.

The women of this class spend the winter in spinning cotton and wool, making carpets, sacks, etc., and in sewing garments for their children and husbands. Young girls are busy in preparing useful articles for their wedding. The dozen or more holidays that come during the year are celebrated by this class in having big dinners, and the women cease from the heavy burdens of their labor for the day and attempt to beautify themselves after the fashion of the women of the higher classes with paint and finery. Their taste not being cultivated in that art they often make themselves more hideous than beautiful.

CHAPTER VII.

THE MOSQUES AND THEIR SERVICES.

THE mosque is the Mohammedan holy temple or church. There is one in almost every community which has been erected by lords or rich people. In the cities they have some magnificent mosques built of stone and brick. A mosque is divided into several small rooms and two large halls. One hall is for winter service, the other for summer. The summer hall is in the front end of the building, is enclosed with three walls, the front being open. The pillars that guard the entrance to this hall are adorned with artistic designs. The interior walls of the mosque are painted white and on them are inscribed in large letters numerous verses from the Koran. The floors of the halls are not covered with carpets or rugs, as they would be stolen ; but there are cheap mats made of reeds on the floor. There are no chairs, as the worshippers sit on the floor.

It is believed that any man who builds a mosque has remission of his sins. It gives him great reputation, and he is known as a holy and religious man. There are some very old mosques, a few having stood as long as 900 years. In some instances Christian churches have been converted into mosques in times of persecution. In the city of Oroomiah one very fine church was converted into a mosque about 600 years ago. It is a very large building with a high steeple and stands in the heart of the city, surrounded by fine grounds of about three acres. The grounds are surrounded by a high wall, inside of which are rows of small buildings divided into rooms and used by students. These were originally used by the Christians as a kind of university. Even to-day the door facing the east, which Christians entered to worship Jesus, remains. When the Mohammedans took possession of the building a new door was made on the south side facing the holy city of Mecca. Mosques are regarded as holy, and no animal is allowed to step in, especially dogs. If Mohammedans knew that dogs sometimes enter Christian churches, they would despise Christians the more. Jews and Christians are not allowed to enter a mosque. They can only stand before the door and listen solemnly.

The Mohammedans have no bells on their mosques. They say Satan is in the bell, and that its sound is the sound of Satan. Sometimes they stop our bells, saying that Allah will not accept their prayers on account of our bells.

They have no bell, but a man, sometimes a Mool-lah, who ascends to the roof of the mosque three times daily, morning, noon and night, and in a loud voice calls men to prayer. The call is made in the following words: "Allah Ak-par." This means Almighty God and is repeated three times. Then he continues: "Ashuddu-in-nah la il-la-ha ella Allah" meaning, "I testify that there is no god but God. "Ashud-du in-nah Mohammed rus-sool Al-lah," meaning, "I testify that Mahommed is the only apostle of God." "Hay-ya alal sa-lah," meaning "Hasten to prayer." "Hay-ya alal falah," meaning "Hasten to the place of refuge and hope," "Hay-ya alal Kher-ul amal," meaning "Hasten to do good works." The call is concluded by again repeating three times the words, "Allah Ak-par."

The mosque is open day and night, and men may come into prayer at any hour. Friday is holy day and corresponds somewhat to the Christian Sunday. No man is chastised if he works on Friday, but all faithful Mohammedans attend public services on that day. The services in the mosques of the cities are conducted by Muj-ta-hids or high priests. The priest starts to the house of worship when he hears the voice of the Mah-zin calling to prayer from the top of the mosque. He is accompanied by eight or ten servants, besides numbers of worshippers who may fall in line with the holy man. When he enters, the assembled worshippers rise to their feet and remain standing until the priest has seated himself in the pulpit. He will recite from the Koran and tell traditions in a chanting voice. Women are allowed to attend these services, but they are required to sit in one corner of the mosque apart from the men.

SPECIAL SERVICES.

Among Muj-ta-hids two titles are given to those who excel in holiness, viz., Pish-Namaz and Imam-Ju-ma. The former means mediator in prayer; the latter, the prophet of holy Friday. They are indeed more devoted to their faith and at the same time more fanatical in their hatred for Christianity. When one of these priests goes to the mosque he wears a large turban on his head, some of them costing $50, a cloak of fur, a staff with gold or silver handle. He wears a long beard which is painted black. Following him is a procession of from fifty to one hundred men, mostly mollah, or lower class, who are faithful Moslems. Proceeding toward the mosque with slow and solemn tread, he is saluted by the people of all classes along the street by their rising to their feet, crossing the breast with the arms and reverently bowing before him, uttering the words "Sallam ali-Kun Agha," which means "peace be unto you, sir." This service occurs on holy Friday. Sometimes 2,000

PRIESTS AT WORSHIP.

or 3,000 men will be gathered in the mosque. Women are not admitted in these most holy and solemn services. The Muj-ta-hid stands in the front part of the mosque, facing Mecca, and all the audience is back of him. As he advances in the prayer all the people repeat what he prays. They imitate every motion he makes. When he kneels, they kneel. When he puts the ends of his front fingers in his ears, the entire audience does the same. They believe all prayers which are prayed in that way are accepted through his mediatorial prayer.

CHAPTER VIII.

Moslem's Private Prayer and Fasting.

PRAYER.

PRAYER carries the Musselman half way to heaven. There is no salvation by grace or by atonement. Allah forgives his sins only on the condition of good works. Hence it is an obligation with every one to pray. Prayer is not a duty issuing from his love to Allah, but a yoke which binds him against his will. It is reduced to a mechanical act without spirit. The Moslem always washes with cold water before prayer. He will take a jar of water and say,

"Bism Allah," meaning, "in the name of God I do this holy service." Then, dipping his right hand in the water, he rubs his arms from the wrist to the elbow; with the tips of his fingers he will wet his forehead and the inside of his ears, and the surface of his feet. Travelers in the desert use sand as a substitute for water. The worshipper must have a seal of Mecca, which is made of clay and is about the size of a half-dollar. On it are the words, "There is no god but God." Facing Mecca, he puts the seal on the ground, and, standing erect, he raises both hands to his head, kneels to the ground, puts his brow on the seal, then kisses it. Rising to his feet he puts both index fingers in his ears; and also makes numerous other gestures. They have one prayer which is always repeated. They have five stated seasons daily for prayer; day-break, noon, soon after noon, after sunset (to avoid the idea of sun worship) and just before retiring. The general place of prayer is the mosque, but few of the Moslems pray there, as they prefer praying in the streets, open squares and in meadows before mosques, where they will be seen by more men and can better show their piety and integrity. In the midst of his prayer he will stop and speak a few words to the surrounding people as a religious custom, or to revile children whose noise while at play may have interrupted him. A prayer often prayed by faithful Moslems, quoted from the Koran, is a foolish and selfish prayer, and is entirely against the spirit and teachings of our Lord Jesus Christ. It reads: "O Allah, I seek refuge to thee from Satan and all evil spirits. O Lord of all creatures destroy all heathen and infidels, even those who believe in the Trinity, the enemy of our religion. O Allah, make their children orphans, their wives widows, and defile their abodes. Give their families, their households, their women, their children, their relatives, their possessions, their race, their wealth, their lands, and their daughters as a booty to the Moslems, Thy only people, O Lord of all creatures." Every word is against the blessed teachings of our Lord, who said: "Love your enemies, bless them that curse you, do good to them that hate you, and pray for them which despitefully use you and persecute you."

The Mohammedan religion does not require woman to pray. It is a question if she has the same soul that man has. However, some women among the higher classes and some old widows do pray. But they cannot pray in the most holy mosques on account of their uncleanness, nor in the streets, for they ought not to be seen of men. If they wish to they may pray in their private houses.

While prayer carries a Musselman half way to heaven, fasting carries him to the gate and alms admit him. So fasting and alms are the keys to paradise, and every man must practice them. The Moslems have only one month of fasting, called the ramadhan. Their month begins with the new moon; but sometimes in some parts of the land it is cloudy and they cannot see the moon. So men will be appointed by the government throughout all the empire to watch carefully for the new moon, sometimes from the peaks of mountains. When she is discovered telegrams are sent announcing the beginning of the fast on the morrow. They will fast from one hour before sunrise to one half hour after sunset, or till it becomes too dark for a man to discriminate between red and black thread. During this time they abstain from eating, drinking and smoking. The poor class work till noon. The rich do not work at all. The most of the day is spent in reciting the Koran, praying and sleeping. Christians cannot eat in the street, for the Moslems might long to eat, too, or even take a taste, and thus break their fast. Boys and girls above eight years must fast, while sick men are not compelled to during this month. However, when they recover, they are required to fast thirty days as soon as they are able. They do not converse much in the day, but wear a sad countenance. They do not allow a Christian to speak to them. At morning and evening in the cities a cannon is fired for the beginning and ending of the fast. During this month much alms is given. The lords and princes especially send meals from their table. They believe fasting and giving secure absolute forgiveness of sins and admittance to heaven. The night is changed to a feast. They eat and drink and converse till twelve o'clock. Then they retire, but are up again at three and eat and drink till one hour before sunrise. Death among them occurs most often in that month, because many eat too much. So many different meals hurt their stomach and they fall sick and die. The Mohammedans say they go to heaven, for its gates are open during this month for Musselmans. Hundreds of them eat everything they want, and at any time of the day. They do not believe in fasting. But they must be careful that the high priest does not catch them breaking the fast, for he would punish such offence severely. The writer has seen many Mohammedans eating in this month. They would eat and smoke in their houses and then wash out their mouths and tell everyone they were fasting. Thousands fast either for their own glory or from fear of men.

CHAPTER IX.

THE PILGRIMAGES.

ISLAM'S religion has many holy places, and it is the duty of every Mohammedan to visit these shrines unless circumstances hinder him. Pilgrimages secure not only forgiveness of sins, but a great reputation as well. Of all Mohammedan shrines there are four most remarkable. Medina is the first. It was the birthplace of Mohammed. Here he lived till he was six years old, when his mother, Amina, died. A slave girl faithfully nourished him and took him to Mecca. But his last days were spent in Medina. When he was dying in the arms of Ayesha, Omar asked him: "Prophet, where do you wish us to bury you?" He answered: "Throw the rein of the bridle on my camel's neck, and I believe the angel Gabriel will come and direct her where to go. There bury me." They did so. His camel started off, but soon stopped and would not proceed further. So they buried Mohammed there, and a magnificent mosque stands above his grave. This building is adorned with silver and gold, and Mohammedans worship it.

The second place is Mecca. This city is the most holy for all the Mohammedan world. Here is the old temple of the Arabs, the Kaaba, which was converted by Mohammed into a mosque. It has been rebuilt many times by the rich kings of Islam. This mosque is among the seven wonders of the world, and is not inferior in beauty and cost to Solomon's temple. Outside at the gate is a black stone which the ancient Arabs worshipped before Mohammed. Some said the stone was cast out of paradise with Adam; others that it was cast down from heaven. Upon it Abraham offered Isaac. The worshippers held a tradition that if anyone should place a smooth stone on this holy stone and it should stick fast he should have the wish of his heart. Many childless women use this means to find if God will give them a child. Near the mosque is the well of Ab Zimzim, *i.e.*, living water. Mohammedans claim Abraham, Hagar and Jacob quenched their thirst at this well. Jacob and other patriarchs, they say, watered their sheep here. Many pilgrims have tried to assure the writer that the mosque of the Kaaba was originally built by the angel Gabriel. There are two hundred million Moslems scattered throughout the world, and each of them turns his face toward this mosque and prays five times daily.

The third place is Karballa. This city holds the second place in sacredness in the estimation of the Mohammedans. It is situated in Asiatic

Turkey, near the famous city of Baghdad, where Saleck and Katispon once flourished, ancient towns of the Christian Nestorians. Here their patriarch dwells who ruled over all the Nestorian Church. After the death of Mohammed his four caliph successors overthrew these places and took them from the Nestorians. Later a battle took place here between these caliphs and the grandchildren of Mohammed to decide which should be at the head of the new religion. The caliphs were successful; the grandchildren being slain. They were buried here and upon their graves was reared a magnificent mosque. Like that of Mecca, this, too, is adorned with gold and silver. Hundreds of rich men from all parts of Persia give large offerings for this temple. Karballa has different meanings. Some translate it the place of danger, some the place of mourning, some the place of the killing of martyrs, others the place of those holy men. Here in this city is the pope of all Persia—they call him prophet. In his hands is all the power of his religion, and he has more power than the king. Everything he commands they must do, even to the killing or massacring of all the Christians. The king must do him formal reverence.

The fourth place is Mashhad. This city is situated in the northeast part of Persia, in the state of Khorason, near the Caspian Sea. This is the most holy city in Persia. Here are buried many famous persons, as the grandchildren of Mohammed. This mosque is more rich than Mecca and Karballa. The dome is gilded with gold outside and inside. Generally each king of Persia makes expensive presents, but the most remarkable event in this connection was two hundred years ago. Nadirshah, a powerful king of Persia, he that conquered India and despoiled Delhi of its treasures, made a present to this temple of a crown of gold, adorned with precious stones. They say at night it is like the Electricity Building at the Columbian Exposition. They call it Mashhad-Mokaddas, meaning holy. It is a place of martyrs. No Christians or Jews are permitted to reside in this city. In the thirteenth century this was the cathedral of the archbishop of the Nestorians.

PILGRIMAGES TO THE HOLY PLACES.

Mohammedan law commands all to go to these holy places. The books of ceremony emphasize the importance of such pilgrimages. The hope of remission of sins is given to all visitors, and they are thereafter called by a different name from ordinary men. Everyone has confidence in them; and sometimes for a witness they call from this class of men. Their law is, every man able must go and God will be merciful to his family, and afterward he will be rich. Everyone who refuses to go is not a true Moslem and does not love his religion.

PREPARATION FOR THE JOURNEY.

Before going on this journey many fast and pray. They must repent of every sin, and sometimes one sees men praying in various ways, and it is easy to see that they are preparing for a pilgrimage. They put on a sorrowful countenance and walk about sadly—all of which is merely for vain-glory. Every day they must wash and cleanse themselves and go to the mosque. If they are at enmity with any man, they must first be reconciled before their journey will be recognized. Some days before starting some Say-yids, descendants of Mohammed, who wear a blue turban and are considered most honorable and holy men, who do not work, who are not punished for any violation of law, will ride on blue horses with long spears in their hands. They will walk in the streets crying in a loud voice to all those who are to make a pilgrimage to prepare themselves and be ready on a certain day. Together with this command is uttered words of comfort and encouragement. They tell the people not to fear. God will send, for the sake of Mohammed, His angels and prophets, riding on blue horses, to deliver them from all robbers and thieves. Yet many do die on this pilgrimage at the hands of desperate characters of the desert or mountains.

ALMS-GIVING.

One month before starting each man must give according to his ability for alms. They are besieged by the others to prepare food and drink for feasts. If a man is rich the demand is repeated. Before starting the pilgrim goes to the leader to inquire what is necessary for him to do and how to do it, that his pilgrimage be accepted. The priest will say, if the man is rich, "You found a mosque." If a man is poor a smaller amount of money is required. The very poor are commanded to fast from ten to forty days. Those who make their pilgrimage on horseback scatter money on the way for the benefit of the beggars and the poor. As the pilgrim sets out he is accompanied by friends for some distance as a mark of honor to the faithful Islam. Before the band of pilgrims the leader rides calling out in a loud voice, "Salawat."

CARRYING THE DEAD.

Their law requires that not only the living, but also the dead, shall go to these places. The dead are sometimes carried to the sacred cities forty years after burial. Sometimes when a stingy man dies who has not gone on a pilgrimage in his lifetime, he exacts a promise from his relatives that a certain amount of his money will be used to carry his body to a holy city. If this promise is not kept, the priest will compel his relatives and heirs not only to restore the specified sum for sacred purposes, but more. When the poor man is about to die, he administers an oath to his relatives that after his death his body shall at some future time be taken to Karballa. As a reward for this service, the relatives will be blessed of God and made rich. The dead are buried in a box so that at some appointed time the remains may be exhumed and transferred to a new box and strapped to the back of a horse and carried to the holy city. It matters not if the body has decayed. If the bones remain it is not too late for the pilgrimage. If the deceased has been very poor and his friends cannot take him in person, they hire strangers to do it. Thus one may see the caravans with hundreds of horses—sometimes thousands—with the boxes of dead strapped to their backs on their way to the holy places.

MOTIVE IN PILGRIMAGES FOR THE DEAD.

The object of these trips is to secure heaven for the dead. Their religion teaches that all who die in a holy city or who are buried there find a home in heaven. Some say God has a multitude of spiritual camels with riders who will come and carry the dead bodies to heaven. If you say to them, "Flesh and bones cannot inherit the holy place of God," they will answer, "Their spirit is taken to heaven, not their body." Others will say, "The bones are not the original ones, but likenesses of them." Others say, "it is an honor to the prophets who are buried in the holy city for other dead men to be buried there." At an appointed time after burial it is believed that the dead will rise and bow to the tombs of the prophets. This is the manner of their worship: Those who go to Medina must arrive before a certain day, because on that particular day their worship is commenced. For two or three days various ceremonies are performed, such as fasting, prayer, purification and washing of their bodies. When these are concluded, on the fourth day, they array themselves in a special robe for worship. Without any covering on their feet they walk around the mosque seven times. When they enter the mosque they bow themselves before the tomb of Mohammed. After this bowing they walk seven times around the tomb of the prophet. They then kneel down and kiss the tomb, at the same time placing such money upon it as they can spare. Upon leaving the mosque a ram is killed as a sacrificial offering. On that day more than one hundred thousand sheep are killed in that small city. This together with the warm sun beating on the blood of the victims gives rise to the most fearful of all scourges, cholera. In Karballa, Medina and Mashhad worship is conducted in this manner.

THE FEMALE PILGRIM.

The law requires that females also go to these holy places. Girls at every age are allowed to go, also children. Widows under fifty years are not accepted as pilgrims; first, because of their probable desire for marriage, and second because the law says no woman must undertake a pilgrimage alone, for thus they would expose themselves to men. So in order to go some marry for the occasion. The husband accompanies them hither, and upon returning either divorces them or keeps them as wives or concubines.

THE RETURN OF THE PILGRIMS.

Those who went to Mecca from certain parts before trains began to run in the East consumed a year or more in their journey, but now it takes only six or eight months. Those going to Karballa take from three to five months, likewise those going to Mashhad. Every band of pilgrims when returning to their own city will send a messenger about ten days ahead to announce that in so many days a band of pilgrims will appear in the city. On the day of their arrival many hundred men will meet them several miles from the city. The Sayyids ride before them crying "salawats." Friends and relatives kill lambs as a sacrifice before them. This sacrifice is a holy thing and no man can touch it till its blood is shed; but, when it is beheaded, it belongs to God, and the strongest man takes it for his own. This being a sacred thing, all are very anxious to partake of it. The weak will do all they can to keep the strong from carrying the sacrifice away. So there is always quarrelling when the pilgrims return. The acquaintances of the pilgrims will come and say, "My portion be as thy portion. Blessed art thou. May your pilgrimage be accepted," and the pilgrim will answer, "God grant that you may also go to this Holy Place and receive remission of sin." Women will sometimes cut pieces from the pilgrim's garments, which are supposed to be holy. At the pilgrim's home many sheep are killed and a variety of fine meats are cooked. People gather there to eat and drink, and they say to the host, "God bless your pilgrimage." He will answer, "May the prophet give you success, and grant that you, too, may visit the Holy Place."

It is evident from the above descriptions that there is no place in Islam for peace of conscience or absolute assurance of heaven. The writer has often asked of Mohammedans: "Have you any hope of heaven?" They say, "We don't know; God knows." "Yes; God knows everything, but what do you say of your hope?" He will reply, "I have no hope—but God is merciful."

Many of them would receive Christ if there was freedom of worship. There are even now some true Christians among the Moslems, who worship secretly, like Nicodemus. Let us pray that God will open the way of freedom for them.

CHAPTER X.

THE SHIITE MOSLEM'S MU-HAR-RAM.

WHEN Mohammed was dying he announced, against his will, that Abbubaker, his father-in-law, was his rightful successor. It was his real desire to be succeeded by Ali, his son-in-law, but he saw that Abbubaker had a much wider influence than Ali. In the next generation, after the four caliphs, or chief disciples of the head of the faith, and Ali had died, there arose divisions in the church. Hassan and Hussein, sons of Ali, claimed to be the rightful caliphs after the death of Abbubaker. They contended that their grandfather had made Abbubaker caliph because he was old and faithful, and therefore that that office should not descend to his children. A great body of Moslems followed them. One of them, Hassan, was too timid to push his claims. His death came soon from a dose of poison administered to him by some of his enemies. The energetic young Hussein continued to assert his claims, but he had no army. With seventy men, mostly relatives, he started for a fortified city, but was surrounded by the army of Yazid. Taking shelter in a cave, beneath a huge rock, Hussein and his followers defended themselves for three days and three nights. At last they were driven to desperation by hunger and thirst. Drawing their swords they came out and met an army of several thousand men. After a brief contest Hussein and his men were overcome. Hussein was captured alive. The Shiite Moslems of Persia say that when Hussein was taken before the chief captain for execution, he was very thirsty and asked for a drink of water before being beheaded. But this request was not granted, and he was executed with his thirst unquenched. In memory of this tragedy there may now be seen walking the streets of Persian cities every warm summer day men carrying a bottle or jar of water, and crying aloud: "Sakkaw, sakkaw" (their name), and giving water to any who may be thirsty, in the name of Hussein. Moslems take this drink in a cup carried by the sakkaw, but a Christian must furnish his own cup or drink from the palms of his hands. If offered one or two cents the sakkaw will take it, but he never asks for money.

The killing of Hussein and his followers occurred in the month called Muharram. This entire month and ten days of the following month are observed as a time of lamentation for Hassan, Hussein and their followers who were slain. During this period every man, woman and child of the Shiite Moslems are under obligations to wear black garments. The last ten days of Muharram are observed in a fanatical spirit, as a revival of religion. This period is called Ashara, meaning ten days. The first seven days are for preparation. The mosques will be crowded with men and women. The Mas-ya-Khans, or revivalist priests, are in charge of these services. Followed by a large procession, this priest goes to the mosque and mounting a high pulpit preaches to large crowds. His general theme is tragic tales, stories of martyrs, the manner of their death, their last utterances and the wailing and moaning of their friends and relatives. Often in the concluding words of a pathetic story, the entire audience, sometimes numbering thousands, will be deeply moved, and, slapping their foreheads with the palms of their hands, will cry aloud to give vent to their emotions. The mosques cannot accommodate all the worshippers during this period, so some parts of a street are laid with carpets and rugs, where the people sit while listening to preaching.

The last three days are the most solemn. All the stores of the city are closed and no business of any kind is transacted. At an early hour on these days the whole population, except the old men and women, who stay at home to take care of young children, gather around the mosques. In and near the mosque a national and a religious emblem are carried on a pole by strong men. These are quite heavy, and the standard-bearers change every few minutes. Headed by these emblems, the large crowd, often numbering 3,000 to 6,000 people, will march through the streets. Each company visits from one mosque to another. Passing through the streets the men bearing the national and religious emblems are followed by musicians playing mournful dirges with such instruments as drum, flute and cymbals. Surrounding the musicians are hundreds of men marching with bare breasts, shouting "Hassan, Hussein Hassan, Hussein," and pounding upon their breasts with bare hands. Following them is another band surrounding a Say-yid, a descendant of Ali, and all of them are shouting "Hassan, Hussein," and beating their breasts. Next in the procession comes a band of ascetic darwishes, wearing neither hat nor shoes nor other garments than a pair of pants, when the weather is mild. Holding in their hands a whip about two feet long and one or two inches in diameter, made of small iron strands, they beat their bare shoulders and back with the same as they march, shouting, "Yahu, Yamalhu," which are names of their god. Following comes another band of darwishes bearing in one hand a knotty club to which is fastened nails, bits of brass, etc. With the other hand they beat their breasts, as they repeat the cry of the preceding band. These worshippers torture the flesh by beating it thus and bruise it black. The procession is completed by a crowd of boys and girls and women following. The marching commences early in the morning and continues till eleven; is taken up again at two in the afternoon and continues till six o'clock.

The greatest demonstration of all occurs on

the last of the ten days. At sunrise the crowds of former days gather around the mosques to start again on the marches. On this day there are also fresh recruits. In front of the mosque is a band of 50 to 100 men and boys of 13 to 40 years of age. They are bareheaded, and uniformed with a white shirt over the other clothing that reaches to the feet. Held in the right hand before each one is a two-edged sword. The left hand rests on the belt of the soldier next in front. The leader, standing at the head of the band, recites their creed: "Allah is God and the only God. Mohammed is the prophet of God and Ali is his vicar." All the band repeats this creed. Immediately the leader smites his own brow with his sword, and this act is imitated by all his followers. Soon the faces and white clothing of the men are red with blood. Bleeding, they go marching through the streets, shouting: "Hassan Hussein," and waving their swords in harmony with step and voice. Their route can often be traced by drops of blood in the streets. When zeal reaches a high pitch, the blows are repeated on their brows. Fearing that these zealous young men may lose all regard for life, and inflict upon themselves mortal blows, relatives or friends frequently walk near with long sticks in hand to hinder them from such deeds.

This band first marches to the court-house to be seen by the governor. Every band has a right to ask the governor for the freedom of some one prisoner, and these requests are always granted, no matter what the crime of the imprisoned. These bleeding men are as martyrs, and would go direct to heaven if death resulted from these self-inflicted wounds. After the parade ends, the bloody shirts of these men are divided among their friends and kept as holy relics. The men who compose these bands are usually the most wicked in the community. They go through these ceremonies for the remission of sins, and to redeem themselves in the eyes of others; but they usually continue in their wickedness as time goes on.

Another important feature of the last day in the procession, is a richly decorated hearse containing a coffin, in which lies a man representing the corpse of Hassan. Beside the coffin sits a woman, the widow of Hassan, dressed in sackcloth, and her head covered with mud. Following the hearse are three beautiful Arabian horses, finely saddled and harnessed, with a flake of gold, embedded with pearls, on their foreheads. On two of them are seated two girls, representing the daughters of martyrs. The tops of the girls' heads are covered with mud and straw. The third horse is riderless to remind one of the missing martyr. Following next is a large number of women, boys and girls and some men, all with yokes about their necks, their hands chained behind them, seated on horses and mules. These are to represent the captives taken by Yazid, the captain who killed Hussein. Near them are men in helmets to represent the soldiers of Yazid. They are armed with whips and are driving these women and children of Moslems into captivity. Next in line may be seen false heads, raised aloft on poles, representing Yazid, Mawya, and other ancient enemies of Hussein. Boys and men gather around them, spitting at and reviling them. Gathered, all the sword-bearers, chain-strikers and the many men beating their breasts, they make a great crowd and tremendous noise. The bystander is struck with horror when two fanatical bands meet, each trying to excel the other in self-mutilation. Then are frightful gashes cut; the thumping of chains on bruised bodies and the pounding of breasts is heard louder than before. With an upward sweep of the right arm every man cries in a loud voice: "Ya Ali, Ya Ali!" as the companies pass each other.

At 4 p.m. on the last day the marching ceases, and the throng halts by some tents pitched in the middle of a public square. The population of the city is gathered round about.

There is not even standing room for all, and hundreds or thousands of people are gathered at windows or on housetops near by. Perhaps 20,000 people are present. The sword and chain strikers approach the tents and with a shout of victory utter the names of Ali, Hassan and Hussein, then set fire to the tents and burn them and their contents to the ground. They imagine that their enemies were in those tents, and now that they have been destroyed it is a time of great rejoicing. The marching clubs disband and the active ones are soon found at the mosques drinking sharbat, a sweet drink, as a sort of reward for performing their religious duties.

SINGERS.

The closing hours of the last day are given to the singing of poems by the best musicians, gathered at the mosques. The singing band usually numbers from twenty to thirty men. They sing poems about the last utterances of Hussein and other martyrs, or about the sayings and weeping of the relatives of these martyrs.

It is not very safe for Christians to mix with the crowds on these last days, unless in company with some honest Mohammedan. If one is seen laughing at the ceremonies he is apt to be beaten by some one whose fanatical spirit is thoroughly aroused. Our missionaries sometimes ask the privilege of using a roof by which the procession passes. This is always granted. The three nights are considered holy and the most religious Moslems do not retire until midnight. Services are held in the mosques, reciting traditions. The audience is composed of men only. It would not be safe for the women to attend, owing to the wickedness of the men. The audience is frequently deeply moved by the tragic tales, and weep angry tears. They curse and revile their enemies and their enemies' wives and daughters. The last night is called watch-night, and many Moslems do not even slumber during the night. It is holy night in which Hussein and other martyrs were buried in their tombs. It is a dishonor, and even a sin, for them to go to bed without meditation on their prophets. In the mosque services the people shout: "O Hassan and Hussein, let my soul be a sacrifice for thee." They believe the observance of that night is absolute remission of sins; that the gates of heaven are open to all believers for the sake of the martyrs. Some pious Moslems preserve the tears of that night in small bottles, as it is believed they will cure disease when applied to the brows of sick men. These tears are prized as a most holy relic. The Musselman says: "Even David the prophet believed in the efficacy of tears when he wrote in the Psalms, 'Put thou my tears in Thy bottle, O God.'"

On the last night many Shiite Moslems walk to the mosque in bare feet, wearing sackcloth. Often a governor or lord, accompanied by 40 to 100 servants, all barefooted, will be seen slowly treading their way toward a mosque. Wearied by the great exertions of the past ten days it is difficult to keep awake during the last night; so many men will be seen coming out of the mosques during the night to walk around and keep awake. At daybreak these solemn ceremonies end. In all these ten days of special religious services not one word is said in condemnation of sin. There is no moral teaching. Nothing is taught about man's duty to God, or his duty to his fellow-men. Nothing is said to strengthen his character, to make him a purer and nobler man. The only teaching is in tragic tales of martyrs; the only inspiration is hatred to enemies.

Compare this religion with that of our blessed Saviour, Jesus Christ, God-man. He gave His life for all nations, even His enemies. He calls mankind to sacrifice, but it has a practical object: that they may be purer and live a higher and nobler life. Christianity is as the sun shining in its fulness, while Mohammedanism, in its ignorance and superstition, is as the darkness of midnight.

CHAPTER XI.

Heaven and Hell.

HEAVEN.

MOHAMMED declared in the Koran that there are seven heavens. Above all is the heaven for prophets, martyrs, those who die in battle for religion's sake, and for angels. Chief among all in this heaven is Mohammed, mediator between God and believers. The other heavens will be inhabited by believers, the degree of piety and integrity determining to which heaven they shall go.

Heaven was pictured as an earthly paradise. There are beautiful gardens, vineyards, green pastures, fresh fountains, the river of living water, many bathing pools of glass, a palace of marble and glass, ornamented with pearls and diamonds. The trees bear fruit continuously, some in blossom, others ripe with fruit. Prominent are the palm and grape, fruits which were favorites of Mohammed while on earth. Choice fruits grow in abundance and on low trees, so that a man can stand on the ground and eat of the fruit. Each vine bears 7,000 clusters of grapes, and every grape contains 7,000 gallons of juice. The pastures are eternally green, and in them grow many thousand varieties of flowers of exquisite odors. There are no animals in heaven, as they are not needed. There will be no dogs, cats, swine, nor unclean birds, as eagles, hawks, and buzzards. But there are millions of brilliantly plumaged birds, whose melodies continually ring through heaven. The walls and gates of heaven are as described in the 22nd chapter of Revelation.

Believers will spend eternity in the joys of luxurious life in paradise, amidst blooming gardens and beautiful virgins. To an ordinary believer will be given 72 houries, or female angels. These creatures are described in the Koran as being fair, with rosy cheeks, black eyes and in blooming youth. Such beauty the eyes of men have not seen on earth. Martyrs and more pious men have more than 72 houries, the number increasing in proportion to the believer's prominence. The believer will sit under a fragrant tree in a golden chair, or lie on a golden cot, while birds overhead sing wonderfully sweet. His fairies will be about him and offer him choice unfermented wine in a golden cup on an emerald tray. Such is the Moslem's heaven.

These were the promises with which Mohammed aroused the enthusiasm of his followers. Fanatical zeal has been so enkindled in men that many thousands have perished in an effort to spread these doctrines throughout the world.

Saints will live nearer to Allah than ordinary believers and will have conversation with him. No people can enter heaven unless they be Moslems. The gate to heaven is reached by a bridge. This bridge is as narrow as a hair, and only believers can walk it. When a soul approaches the gate it finds Fatima, the daughter of Mohammed, standing there. She asks him to recite the creed: "Allah is the only God, and Mohammed is his prophet." If repeated, the soul enters heaven; if not, with a breath Fatima blows him off the bridge and he falls into hell, the regions below.

HELL.

As there are seven heavens according to degree of integrity of believers, even so there are seven hells. Gehenna is beneath the lowest part of the earth and the seas of darkness. It is a place of fire, as a great ocean without limits. It burns with brimstone and like materials. There are thousands of terrible flames and bad smells. Satan is there with all infidels, Christians, Jews, fire-worshippers and apostate Mohammedans. The torture of the latter will be worse than the torture of others. There are in hell thousands of wild animals, as lions, tigers, vipers and serpents. Every lion has in his mouth 7,000 teeth, and every tooth has 7,000 different stings or poisons. So with the tiger and serpents. Every viper has 7,000 tails and on every tail 7,000 stingers, and every stinger contains 7,000 kinds of poison. The common drink of the inmates of hell is poison drunk from iron cups. Their meals will be the flesh of animals and even their own flesh. Satan and his servants will torture them with spears and swords of iron. There will be no rest for them day or night. Men and women will gnash their teeth against their own children. All will be weeping, cursing and blaspheming. Hell is surrounded by walls of iron over which none can escape.

CHAPTER XII.

MATRIMONY.

MARRIAGE among Assyrians is considered as sacred as the ordination of priests, but is subordinate to or less sacred than the sacrament of the Lord's supper or baptism. Therefore marriage is a solemn service and the rules relating to it are very strict. Engagements for marriage are made by the parents of the con-

NESTORIAN WEDDING.

tracting parties rather than by the young people themselves. Girls are strictly forbidden speaking of or referring to marriage in the presence of their parents or brothers. If a young man loves a young lady, he does not ask his parents' consent to marriage, but tells his aunt or married sister about what cupid has done for him. This news is soon conveyed to his mother, and then it is proper for her to call on the mother of the young lady. If not already acquainted with the young woman, this visit will give her an opportunity to form an opinion of her. If that opinion is favorable, all is well and the matter will be further considered. But if the opinion is unfavorable she returns home and tells her son that she is not pleased and does not want him to marry this girl. This method must be resorted to as the girls and boys in Assyria do not have an opportunity to associate as they do in America. Mothers always advise their girls not to walk with boys and young men, and custom does not permit it. Therefore, if she meets a young man in the street, she bows, and perhaps blushes a little, as she passes. If lovers are passing each other, custom does not allow them to stop and converse, but it does allow the young man to telegraph his message of love with a wink. Several months usually elapse between the engagement and marriage.

The method of making an engagement is quite different from that of Americans. After a mother has assured herself that a certain girl whom her son fancies would make him a good wife, she, with two or three relatives, will send word to the girl's parents that they will call at a certain time, and stay over night. While there the object of their visit will be made known and the matter discussed. If the girl's parents are ever so willing, they will not give their consent at the first visit, but will take the matter into consideration. The friends are invited to call again in two or three weeks for an answer. A third or fourth visit may be made before a final answer is obtained. At the last visit the father of the girl says, in reply to a request for an answer, that the girl does not belong to him. He says he gave her to his brother. The brother then says he gave her to his sister, etc., until the person is reached who can give her away. This man rises and says, "I give our daughter to Mr. and Mrs. ——— as a handmaiden." The question now being settled, refreshments are served and the company rejoices until a late hour. Sometimes the foregoing proceedings are witnessed from an opening in the roof by the young man who is most interested and who is anxiously awaiting the result. During the period of the betrothal, the young man is allowed to make but one visit. He is not allowed to kiss his betrothed until after mărriage. The Assyrian idea of a virgin is a pure maiden who is not married nor has ever been kissed by any man.

Two weeks before the wedding the young man's parents make another call to settle the amount of dowry with which to purchase wedding garments for the bride. The wedding feast lasts two or three days. On the last day a company of the groom's friends go to bring the bride. Dressed in her wedding garments, and seated on a fine horse she is taken to the groom's home. The company make merry on the way with music of drum and flute, and dancing. The horse is stopped about fifty yards from the house, and the groom appears on the roof of his father's house with three red apples in his hands. Kissing each one he tries to throw it over the bride. When the apples strike the ground there is a crowd of boys ready to scramble for them, as there is a superstition that the lucky boy will be the next to marry. The bride now goes to her new home.

The wedding ceremony, which is performed by a minister and a deacon, is taken largely from the Bible. It lasts about two hours, during which time the bride and groom remain standing. The bride's dress covers her body and face from view except her forehead. She wears a crown and is called a queen. The groom wears a high feather on his crown, a sash around his chest and is called a king. For two months after the wedding they are called king and queen. They do no work during this time but visit and take life easy.

MOSLEM MARRIAGES.

The marriage ceremony of the Mohammedans takes place about a week before the formal wedding. It is very simple. Representatives of the contracting parties go to a priest and get two ceremonial letters, one for the bride, the other for the groom. In them is stated the sum necessary for the groom to pay, if he ever divorces the woman. It further states that it is the groom's duty to love this woman and all other women that he may marry thereafter. That it is the bride's duty to love the groom and no one else.

The prevailing low regard for woman grows out of the teaching of Mohammed. Among his last words he charged husbands not to place any confidence in their wives. He stated that they had been the cause of much of the crime and misery in the world.

When a Moslem goes out with his wife he is disgraced if she goes before or even beside him;

she should follow. A man can marry four wives, but can divorce any one of them at any time. But a woman cannot get a divorce from her husband. A man is angry when his wife gives birth to a girl babe, and his friends fear to break the news to him. One man was known to be so angry when his fourth daughter was born, that he did not speak to his wife for three months. The mother of a son is loved the more, and the first person who breaks the news to the father is given a present.

If a man murders his wife he may be fined a sum of money, but can't be executed, because woman is not equal to man. The question as to whether a woman has a soul is sometimes discussed. Men do not salute women in meeting them, but women are expected to bow their heads to men.

PART III.

CHAPTER I.

THE ROYAL FAMILY.

THE present dynasty is called the Kajar dynasty. It began with Agha Mohammed Khan, who was taken captive by the enemy when he was a child, and all of the prominent members of the family excepting children were slain. Agha Mohammed Khan, then a boy six years of age, was made a eunuch by the new king to serve in his harem. But at the age of twenty or twenty-five he escaped from his master and returned to his relatives and former friends. Collecting a force he attacked the king's army, and after several engagements overthrew the king and took possession of the throne. As a ruler he was very cruel to his enemies, but very kind to his officers and subjects. One night while resting in his tent two servants or subordinate officials in an adjoining tent quarrelled and awakened the king with their noise. This angered him, and the next day he ordered that both of them be beheaded. The following night, before the time for execution had come, the two condemned men formed a plot with some other officials who hated their ruler's cruelty, to kill the king. This plot was successfully carried out. The king's nephew, Futteh Ali, became his successor. He became one of the most noted kings of Persia, and was called the king of kings. Futteh Ali had several sons, one of whom, Abbas Mirza, was chosen as crown prince. This prince died in early manhood. He left a son, Mohammed by name, who afterwards became king. After Mohammed, the late Nasiraldinshah became king, and was assassinated May 1st, 1896. Nasiraldin was a good king, and did more for Persia than any ruler during the past 700 years. He made three visits to Europe and gathered many modern ideas which he wished to introduce in his kingdom. He organized a postal system connecting all the prominent towns and cities of Persia. Telegraphic communication was also established. He built roads between important towns and cities and detailed soldiers as guards where the roads passed through sections infested with robbers. This king reigned forty-eight years. A year ago he became a victim of a fanatical Bobe, a new religious sect. The assassin took the king's life while the latter was worshipping in the most holy place of a mosque. Nasiraldin left four sons. The eldest is named Zelli Sultan. He is a highly educated and powerful man. The second son, Mozafferedden, succeeded his father, and is now king of Persia. The third son is governor of the capital. The fourth son is a youth of twelve years.

Before the death of the late king, Zelli Sultan, his first son, began making secret preparations to usurp the throne. When the plot was learned, the son was stolen from his home one night and taken before the king. All implements of war prepared by him were confiscated, and he was sentenced to death. But high officials interceded for the son, and the sentence was changed to that of blinding him. When the hour came for putting out the prince's eyes, the king was moved by the young man's beauty, and said there was not a handsomer pair of eyes in all his empire, and that he would not destroy them. Therefore Zelli Sultan's punishment was changed to three years' imprisonment. At the expiration of the term, the king gave him solemn warning that any further attempt at usurpation would be punished by death.

I have often been asked why the first son did not take the throne instead of the second. The reason is this: The king had several wives, but the first one was a princess from his own tribe, and is called the queen. Her first son must be successor to the throne. Therefore Zelli Sultan was not eligible to the throne, as his mother was not a princess.

The present Shah is a man who has a strong desire to rule in peace. He tolerates all religious beliefs, even though they differ from his own. He is loved by all classes of people, and all religious sects because he is kind and considerate toward them.

The Shah is very friendly toward the Christian missionaries. A few years ago he visited the Presbyterian College, the Ladies' Seminary, and listened to some of the recitations. As an

PRESENT SHAH.

evidence of his friendliness he was a guest at the home of Dr. Cochran, and dined with him. Not every one is so honored, for I have heard that an army officer in that part of Persia offered the Shah £3,000 to take dinner with him, but the invitation was not accepted. The Shah has also visited a Nestorian bishop, who resides in a cottage so humble that some lords would be ashamed to enter it. On the other hand, when he was in our city of Oroomiah he did not visit the homes of any of the Mujtahids, but met these high priests in a mosque by appointment.

Of late years the royal family has been kind to Christians. Nine out of ten cases of cruelty to Christians come from the Mujtahids and the lords. The priesthood is stronger than the government in Persia. Sometimes the king has to give up his ideas to please the priests. For example: The late Shah desired to introduce the modern railroad into Persia, but the priests were bitterly opposed to it, and the king had to give up his plans. When asked why they opposed railroads, one priest gave two reasons: First, our country is weak. If we built railroads, Europeans could run in on us and take our country. Second, it would destroy our religion, and we could not control our wives. If we beat them they could take the train and be in Europe in one day, while now it takes twenty days. Again, some of our women might marry Christians and escape to Europe."

THE KING IN HIS PALACE.

The royal palace is surrounded by high stone walls. The grounds are entered by four beautiful gates. The walls at the sides and above the gates are adorned with the pictures of former kings and brave generals; also decorative carvings of lions, the standards of Persia, and of birds. The grounds are beautifully arranged, all the roads leading to the king's palace in the center, and beautified with ornamental trees and hedges of roses of varied hues. Guarding the entrances to the gates and the roadways that lead to the palace doors are numerous officers of superior rank, those nearest the palace ever standing with drawn swords. When the king sits in judgment he uses the peacock throne, and is surrounded by his six cabinet officers, who are advisers. He is absolute, and may overrule the advice of the cabinet. This body makes the laws of the land. The king appoints the members of his cabinet, the people having no voice whatever in government. When the Shah tires of the routine of governmental duties, his secretary reads to him from Shahnameh, a poetical history of Persian kings. It is one of the king's duties to become very familiar with the history of Persia and her former rulers. When the king retires to his private room at night, the entrance to the room is guarded by two most trusted officials with drawn swords. One of the four gates in the walls around the palace is called the king's gate, as he always enters through it. No other person, be he lord, count, or high official, is permitted to pass through this gate on horseback or in carriage. He must dismount and walk through.

When the king goes from the palace for a hunt or vacation, he is escorted out of the city by a large guard. First, coming down the street will be seen about thirty infantry, bearing each a golden club, and shouting: "Get out! get out!" Whereupon the street is cleared of all traffic that the royal procession may pass. The infantry is followed by about fifty cavalrymen with drawn swords. Next comes ten or a dozen riderless Arabian horses. These horses are beauties, and are adorned with bridles of gold and many precious stones.

HIS TABLE.

The king's table is set with the luxuries of the land. From the time of the purchase until it appears on the table, the food is inspected by two trusted officials, whose duty it is to see that the king is not poisoned. Before the king eats of the food it is further examined by his physician.

TREASURY.

The late Shah left $200,000,000 to his son, nearly half of which was in the form of precious stones and jewelry. Perhaps he has a larger amount invested in precious stones than any other king in the world. His peacock throne, which was brought from Delhi, India, by King Nadirshah, who captured that city about 200 years ago, was prized at $12,500,000 some years ago, and is worth more than that now. It is made of solid gold, and is embedded with diamonds, pearls, and other precious stones. The rug upon which he prays is worth $2,500,000. At the beginning of each new year, seated on the peacock throne, he wears his crown, and all of his officers bow before him and wish him a prosperous reign during the new year. On such occasions his person is covered with many dazzling jewels.

WIVES.

The late Shah had forty regular wives and about sixty concubines. The present Shah has seven wives. The palace in which the king's wives reside is almost as beautiful as the king's palace, near which it is located. A number of soldiers guard the entrance to this palace. There are no men inside the palace except a few eunuch servants. There is also a large number of maid servants therein. When the king has many wives he marries some of them against their will. If he fancies a beautiful daughter of a lord, her parents will frequently marry her to the king in order to get an office or a title. The eunuchs have authority to rebuke the wives of the king. Sometimes a number of the women will playfully resent the eunuch's authority and push him against a wall or knock his high hat down over his eyes. Once they picked an old fellow up and threw him into a pool of water, greatly damaging his fine suit of clothes. At times they give a valuable present to a eunuch, such as a nice robe.

CHAPTER II.

GOVERNOR.

PERSIA is divided into thirteen states. The king appoints a governor over each state; this governor appoints a mayor over each city within his territory. This office is not awarded on the basis of education, ability or worthiness.

but is given to the man who will pay the most money, provided his ancestry is fairly good. Many mayors of cities are related to the royal family. These offices are limited to terms of one year, but many times a mayor is removed before his time is out; the subjects may complain, or some person may bid more money for the office. When a man is appointed mayor of a city, the lords and counts of that city, accompanied by soldiers, will go three miles out of the city to meet the new official. He is greeted with discharges of artillery. These lords ride on very fine Arabian horses, with gold-bitted bridles, and escort the mayor into the city. The new governor of the city admires the fine horses of his lords, and sometimes covets some fine steed, and before his term expires finds a way to get possession of it by helping the lord out of some trouble.

If the new mayor is a prince, all prisoners confined in the city jails are taken before him as he enters the city. This is to signify that, as a member of the royal family, he has authority to behead them. The third day after a new mayor has arrived in a city it is customary for lords and counts to visit him with presents of money, golden articles, Arabian horses, etc., as presents. A mayor has from one hundred to three hundred servants. He pays them no salary. Some become his servants for the name, some from fear, and others from choice. Most of these servants get their living from fines and bribes. Some of them are detailed to settle quarrels between men in some village that belongs to the city. This is their opportunity, and they early learn to make the most of it. The mayor has great power. He is judge, sheriff, tax-collector, etc. He has things his own way. When there is an injustice done, there is no other local officer to appeal to.

Prisons. The prisons are frequently cellars, underground, without windows, damp and infested with flies. They are seldom ventilated, and there is no bed nor furniture in them. The government does not feed the inmates. Friends of the imprisoned ones bring bread and throw it to them, and some of this even is sometimes picked up by the jailer and kept for his own nourishment. No men are allowed to visit the prisons, but wives or daughters are allowed to visit their friends if they pay a fee to the jailer. The torture of prisoners is regulated according to the nature of their crimes. The common method of torture for thieves, robbers and murderers is to put the bare foot of the criminal in a vise and squeeze it until he cries in agony. If he gives the jailer some money or promises to give some the next time his friends visit him, the pressure on the foot is lessened. If a man goes to jail wearing good clothes, the jailer often exchanges his own poorer suit for the good clothes.

EXECUTION.

This is done in different ways. A prince from the royal family has authority to behead men. Sometimes when a good friend of the king is appointed governor, the king presents him with a knife. This is a sign, and carries with it authority to behead men. Every prince-mayor or other governor who has been given this authority keeps two executioners. The uniform of this office is a suit of red clothes. These two men walk before the mayor when he goes through the streets. When a condemned man is to be executed he is brought from the cell, hands chained behind, and with a chain about his neck. He is surrounded by a group of soldiers with fixed bayonets. The guilty man has been in a dungeon for several months perhaps. His clothes are in rags, and, having had no bath since first imprisoned, he is very dirty, his hair and beard are long and shaggy. A few steps before him walks the executioner, with blood-red garments and a knife in his hand. Thus they proceed to the public square, and before the assembled crowd the executioner steps behind the kneeling victim and with a single stroke of the keen knife cuts his throat, and another soul takes its flight, having completed its part in the drama of life.

A common mayor who has not the authority to behead, may kill criminals by fastening them to the mouth of a cannon and sending a ball through the body. Another method is to bury the condemned alive in a cask filled with cement, leaving only the head exposed. The cement soon hardens and the victim dies. Sometimes when their crime is not very bad the punishment is the severing of one hand from the body. If the man thus punished should commit a second crime the remaining hand would be severed. If a Mohammedan becomes drunk with wine and gets loud and abusive, he is arrested, and the executioner punctures the partition skin between the nostrils of the drunken man, and a cord of twine, several feet long, is passed through the opening. Then the executioner starts down the street leading his victim. The man soon gets sober, and is very much ashamed. Shopkeepers give the executioner pennies as he passes along the street. Men who quarrel and fight are punished by tying their feet to a post, with the bare soles upward, and then whipping the feet until the flesh is bruised and bleeding, and, frequently, the nails torn from the toes. The victims frequently become insensible under this punishment. One good thing in the laws of punishment is that no Christians or Jews are ever beheaded. The Mohammedans consider the Christian and Jew as being unclean, and think it would be a mean thing to behead them.

Princes, lords and counts are never beheaded. The most severe punishment for a prince is to pluck out his eyes. The method of execution for counts and lords is of two kinds. The king will send a bottle of sharbat to the condemned man, which is given him in the form of a sweet drink, but it contains a deadly poison. He is compelled to drink this, and soon dies. Another form is for the condemned man to be met by a servant from the governor after having taken a bath, and the servant cuts blood vessels in the arm of the condemned until death results from loss of blood.

Thus it will be seen that the contrast in modes of punishment in a Christian nation and a Mohammedan nation is very great. The kind of punishment inflicted on criminals in any country grows out of the prevailing religious belief of that country. A religion that has much cruelty in it will lead a people to torture its criminals. But a nation whose religion is based upon love will deal with its criminals effectively, but as kindly as possible. The writer has visited prisons in both Persia and America, and finds that the contrast between the prisons of the two countries is like the contrast of a palace and a cellar. Prisoners in America ought to be very thankful for the humane treatment they receive under this Christian government.

CHAPTER III.

COUNTS OR LORDS.

THE counts and lords live in luxury. Their title was not obtained by great service to the nation or by high education. It descends from ancestors, and many ignorant and unworthy men bear this title. Wealthy merchants sometimes purchase a title for their sons. The titled class in Persia is very numerous. In one city of 30,000 inhabitants there are more than 500 counts. They own almost all of the land in Persia. In some instances one count owns as much as one hundred villages. All the inhabitants of a village are subjects of the count and they pay taxes to him and also to the king. The men pay a poll tax of one dollar a year; a tax is levied on all horses, cows, sheep and chickens.

The count gets two-thirds of all grain raised by the farmers, and he expects a portion of all fruits raised, which portion is called a present. If this "present" is not large enough to please the count, he has an unfavourable opinion of the subject, and soon finds faults in him and withholds favors. All of the count's work is done by his subjects without pay. When he builds a palace or cultivates a vineyard, he calls upon his subjects to do the work. He punishes his subjects if they rebel or are discourteous to him. Sometimes the punishment is so severe that death is the result. The count collects a large sum of money annually from his subjects in the way of fines—some of them for most trivial offences or discourtesies, and these numerous fines keep the subjects very poor.

The counts are the most immoral class of people in Persia. They are without education, knowing nothing of the sciences, geography, mathematics or political economy, but most of them can read and write the Persian language and know something of Persian history. It is not much wonder that this leisure class becomes immoral, for it is a disgrace for them to do any kind of work, and "Satan finds work for idle hands to do." A count can't keep his own accounts or sell goods in a store. There are no newspapers and magazines circulated throughout Persia to occupy and lead out the thought of the people of leisure hours. No public libraries, and no private libraries except those of a few Persian volumes. The only newspaper published in Persia is an eight-page paper published every three weeks. It does not circulate much outside of the capital city. The Presbyterian Mission publishes a monthly paper about Christian work.

When a subject goes before his lord, he finds the lord seated in his private room before a window. The subject bows before approaching near to the window. When the lord is ready to listen, the subject comes to the window. He usually meets with a frown, and gets replies to his questions in a gruff voice. As a class the counts are not strong physically; they eat and drink too much for their own good.

CHAPTER IV.

CITIES, SCHOOLS AND HOLIDAYS.

THE Persian cities generally are very old and most of them are surrounded by walls about six feet through and twenty feet high. The walls are made of clay, tramped solid by buffaloes or by men. The gates giving entrance to the city are opened during the day from eight o'clock in the morning until night. These walls would not withstand a charge from modern cannon, but they were very useful fourteen years ago when parts of the empire were overrun by about 60,000 Kurds, a tribe of wild nomads. They spoiled the villages wherever they went, but could not take the walled cities. The streets of cities are generally narrow and crooked, and are not paved. The best houses are brick, with stone foundation. Some poor men build homes with sun-dried brick, and still others make the walls of mud. The roof is flat and made of mud, supported by timber. The houses are built adjoining one another, so that men can walk all over the city on the house-tops. This is the common way of travel in winter, when the streets are muddy. In some of the large cities, like the capital, Tehran, and Isphahan and Shiraz, modern paving of streets with stone is being introduced.

On each business street a single line of goods is sold. One will be devoted to dry-goods, another to groceries, another to carpenter shops, another to iron and silver smiths, etc. The streets are from ten to thirty feet in width, and many of them are arched over with brick, so that rain and snow are shut out. Light is let into these enclosed streets by openings in the top of the arch. Camels, horses and donkeys bearing burdens of various kinds of goods may be seen passing through the streets. And in open squares of the city there stands many of these animals belonging to men who have come to the city to buy or sell goods. Before some of the mosques may be seen secretaries or mollahs, whose business it is to write documents in business transactions for which they get from two to fifteen cents.

In buying goods in Persia a stranger is liable to be cheated. It is a custom among dealers to ask two or three times what an article is worth, expecting to come down with the price before making a sale. The silversmiths do some highly skilful work in making rings for the ears and fingers, and belts for the ladies. In all Persia you cannot find a lady selling goods in a store, except in one street where poor old women and widows are allowed to come for a few hours each day to sell such articles as caps, purses, sacks and soaps. Their faces must be covered except the eyes. Only a few women of the lower class are seen in the stores buying goods, and they must not have their faces exposed to view. No Christian can sell fluids, such as milk, oil, syrups or juicy fruits like grapes. It is against the Mohammedan law to buy such things from a Christian. If a Christian wishes to buy any such goods from a Mohammedan he must not touch the same, as the merchant could not thereafter sell it to a Mohammedan.

There are many pick-pockets, both male and female, in the crowded streets. A stranger must beware.

WEIGHTS.

The standard measure is the miscal, 100 of which equals a pound. Four Persian pounds equal one hapta, while it takes five American pounds to equal one hapta. Eight hapta equal one batma. Four batma equal one khancaree. In this measure they weigh raisins, molasses and tobacco. Ten batma equal one load. In this they weigh green wheat, corn, etc. Twenty-five batma equal a kharwar. In this they weigh fuel.

The money is of copper and silver and a very little gold. The following table shows the values of Persian coins:

25	denars	=	½	cent.
50	"	=	1	"
100	"	=	2	"
500	"	=	10	"
1,000	"	=	20	"
10,000	"	=	$2.00	

The bankers sit on small rugs before the shops with boxes of money in their laps. Their chief business through the day is to change money. For changing 20 cents into copper, they charge one cent., and the fee increases in proportion to the amount of the bill changed. Interest in Persia, especially among Mohammedans, is very high, being from 12 to 15 per cent. per annum. But the Synod of the Presbyterian Evangelical Church has a law which forbids any of its members charging more than 10 or 11 per cent.

There are no gas or electric lights in the streets of a Persian city. The mayor appoints an officer, who has a number of assistants, to watch over the city day and night. Every day of the year is given a name by the mayor; as, lion, eagle, Cyrus, fortune, etc. This word is known only to the officials and such persons as may have been given permission to be out at a late hour. If an officer finds a man on the street after 9 o'clock he calls to him to give the name of the night. If he can't do this he is arrested. One of the worst things in a Persian city is the large graveyards, which contain two to five acres of ground. Mohammedans dig up the remains of a dead relative to carry it to a shrine place, and these removals often fill the city with bad odors. These graveyards make excellent hiding places for robbers and thieves. There are many robbers outside of the city walls, and it is very dangerous to go out after night, even a distance of one mile. Victims are usually shot while at a distance, or stabbed and then plundered.

The hammams, or bath-places, are quite numerous in the cities. They are usually well-built brick buildings, and have within two or three pools of water, some hot, others cold. Men can bathe any day in the week except Friday, which day is reserved for women. The charge is three or four cents. Christians cannot enter a Mohammedan hammam, as they are considered unclean.

HOLIDAYS.

The Mohammedans have several holidays. Neither the government nor the priesthood compel observance of these days, but they are usually observed either for the sake of rest, religious profit or amusement. There is, however, one set of holidays—ten days known as Mohrram—that is strictly observed by all faithful Mohammedans. There is also one national holiday generally observed in memory of the beginning of the Persian nation. It is called Newrooz, meaning new day. This name was given by a Persian king in ancient times. Two weeks before this day all stores will be decorated with different kinds of fruits, such as palms, figs, pomegranates, apples, almonds and raisins. Also some fine shawls and rugs are hung before the stores. During these two weeks most people buy of these fruits and prepare for the national feast. On that day nearly every man, woman and child puts on some new garments of clothing and new clothes throughout if possible. People also clean their houses for this occasion. On the evening of Newrooz a table is spread with the finest fruits, and the family will gather around and feast until a late hour in the night. The poor are remembered on these occasions and presents of fruit are sent to them. Christians are also frequently remembered in this way.

SCHOOLS.

There is no system of public or state schools in Persia. There are schools in all large towns and cities which are taught by the priest in a room of the mosque. These schools are voluntary, no person being obliged to send his children. The students pay the priest each from 5 to 25 cents per month. Those who can't pay anything are admitted free. The priest's food is brought to him by the students. The ages of the pupils range from ten to twenty years. These schools are for boys only. There are no schools for girls. If a girl gets any education at all, it must be from a private tutor. In the schools the text-books in history and poetry are in the Persian language, and the Koran and grammar are taught in the Arabic language. Mathematics, geography, the sciences and the history of other nations are never taught. When the pupils are at study they reel back and forth and repeat words loud enough to be heard a block away. They imagine this is an aid to memory. The teacher has authority to punish the students very severely. Sometimes a parent will take his child to a teacher and will deliver him into the gentle keeping of the professor with the remark: "His bones are mine, but his flesh is yours. Teach him, but punish him as you see fit." A post is planted in the school-room, to which a wild boy's feet are fastened, soles upward, and the bottoms are whipped with heavy switches. This punishment is only for the worst boys. For mild offences the teacher raps the student over the head with a long switch, which is always kept in a convenient place or carried in the teacher's hand. The religious teaching consists of quotations from the Koran and traditions about their prophets. The boys are usually very bad about reviling each other and about fighting. The teacher does not protect the weaker, but urges him to return the revilings or the blows he has received. The students of one mosque often attack the students of a neighboring mosque, as they regard them as enemies. The most prominent university of the Shiite Mohammedans is in the shrine place of Karballa. All those who are to become Mujtahids study at this place. In several of the large cities they have schools of higher rank than the ordinary mosque school in which a course of Persian literature is given. It is a pleasure to state that the late Shah, after his visit to some of the universities of Europe, founded a college in the capital city which is called the Place of Science. The French, English and Russian languages are taught, and the study of some modern sciences are being introduced. The college is only for princes and the children of rich people. It is only one flower in a vast wilderness. The problem of Mohammedanism is to keep the common people ignorant, so the priest can continue to rule them. Therefore the priesthood does not favor higher education. Some counts or lords send their sons to Paris to be educated, but the ordinary young men have no opportunities for education.

PART IV.

CHAPTER I.

BOBEISM.

THE Mohammedan religion is to-day divided into about fifty different sects. This division greatly weakens it. The Bobe sect was started by Mirza Mohammed Ali of Shiraz, a city in which reside the most intellectual and poetical scholars of Persia. He began to plan the new religion at the age of eighteen, but did not reveal it until he was twenty-five years old. The foundation of his faith was this: Mohammed, like Christ, taught that the latter days will be a millennium. They have a tradition that when all the prophets had died, or had been killed by their enemies, a son six years of age was, by the direction of Allah, hid in an unknown well. He was to remain there until the time for the millennium. It was believed that he would be the ruler of the Mohammedans in these last days.

He was to lead both his victorious armies and conquer all the world, and Islam would become the universal religion. Mirza Mohammed Ali based his doctrine on this theory, but changed it somewhat. At the age of twenty-five he made several pilgrimages to shrines, such as Karballa, Mecca, and Medina, and then returned to his native town of Shiraz. At first he began to teach his doctrine to his confidential friends and relatives until it was deepened in their hearts. And then he began to preach to the public that he was Mehdeialzaman.

HIS DOCTRINE.

He taught that every age must have its own prophet, inspired from God. He claimed that he was inspired and that he had frequent communications from God telling him how to direct the people. He openly claimed to be Mehdeialzaman. And he taught that the priesthood and the religion were corrupt and that he was appointed to renew them. He did not oppose the Koran, but at the same time said that every age needs a new bible. He claimed to have received a bible from God. This book is called Bayon, meaning exposition. He taught the equality of both sexes and paid homage to woman. He showed that it was against the law of God to marry more than one woman or to keep concubines. Further, it is against the law of society and the happiness of women to marry more than one wife. The law of divorce, which is common among Mohammedans, was not practised by the new sect. The place of woman among them is the same as among Christians. The prophet taught that the spirit of charity ought to be as a flame of fire in the hearts of his followers. He said we cannot please God if we see our brother in need and do not help him; if we pray He will not hear us, if we worship Him He will turn His face away from us. Believing this, the spirit of charity is very strong among them, and they support the needy. The use of wine and all intoxicants is strictly forbidden. They are very kind to people of other faiths who are not Mohammedans; them they hate. Mehdeialzaman preached these doctrines and won many hearts. The converts were generally intelligent and well educated. His doctrine spread through the southern and northeastern parts of Persia. Among his followers were two prominent and attractive persons, Mollah Hussein and Hajee Mohammed Ali. He called them his right and left hand supporters. Another convert of importance was a lady of rare attainments. In poetry she was accomplished, in beauty wonderfully rare, and she was highly educated. She travelled with two assistants from state to state and from city to city preaching the new doctrine. She never met

Bobe, the founder, and knew of him only through letters. She said that God had endowed him with unusual gifts for this holy cause. By the power of her eloquence she made many converts, and was called by her followers Kurratool Alaein, which is a very high title.

PERSONAL APPEARANCE OF BOBE.

In stature he was tall and slender, eyes black: eye-brows, heavy and long; beard, patriarchal. His countenance was very pleasant and attractive. In conversation with high and low classes of people alike he showed himself a servant of all. He was poetical, a great orator and a deep thinker. He wrote many beautiful poems. His epistles to his disciples were philosophical. His words in sermons touched the hearts of men. When orthodox Mohammedans saw that Bobeism was spreading among the people, the priesthood and the government joined in severely persecuting the disciples of the new faith. The disciples were scattered by this persecution to different cities, which resulted in a still greater spread of the new doctrine. At that time the prophet appointed eighteen of his apostles as guards of the faith. Two of them were women, and he requested that this rule be followed in future ages. About this time Bobe and his twelve disciples were arrested in Shiraz and taken to Isphahan. While imprisoned there his doctrines were being rapidly carried on by his followers. He was finally banished to Makoo, an obscure town between Persia and Russia, as it was thought his religion could not spread from such an obscure place. But his doctrine soon prevailed there. At last the priesthood and government decided to bring him to Tabreez to be shot. After his arrival in Tabreez many learned priests came to discuss doctrines with him, but none were able to answer his questions; but his enemies were determined to kill him. Bobe and his twelve disciples were hanged to a wall before the soldiers. Before the order to fire, the disciples were given a chance to save their lives by denying Bobe's faith. Only one denied the faith and was saved. The others asserted that they were willing to die for the truth. When the soldiers obeyed the command to shoot, all the disciples on the wall were killed. But Bobe was not struck by the ball; it struck above his body, cutting in two the rope by which he was suspended. Bobe fell to the ground unharmed and tried to escape through the crowd. He ran into a house, which proved to be the home of an officer, who promptly arrested the fleeing prophet and returned him to the executioner. Before the second shot was fired Bobe was again promised freedom if he would deny his own teachings. He replied that many of the holy prophets of the past died for the truth and that he, too, was willing to die in this holy testimony.

After the killing of Bobe and his disciples, the government issued an edict that the surviving followers who would not deny Bobe should be killed. This happened at the beginning of the reign of the late Shah. Many fanatical Bobes tried to kill the Shah. Soon after the edict one of them shot at the chief ruler of the land, but was killed by a soldier. After this incident fiery persecutions arose against them and about eighteen thousand of their number were killed. The torture inflicted in many instances was very cruel. The more prominent victims were taken to the capital city, stripped of clothing except trousers, and led about the streets while flaming candles were burning away their flesh. Many of them cried allegiance to Bobe to the last. The heroic death of the fanatical Bobes had the effect on many prominent men in the capital of making them believers in Bobe. After the great massacre, which occurred in 1850, the believers in Bobe held their faith in secret. Eighteen men, whose names were not generally known, were appointed guardians of the faith, and one very learned young man was appointed to take Bobe's place. His title is

Baha and he resides in Akra, a small city in Turkish territory. Even to-day they are very earnest in spreading their religion, but their work is done in secret. Their apostles go from place to place and are known by a secret sign.

The enmity between them and the orthodox Mohammedans has been very severe. From the killing of Bobe until the present time they have been trying to kill the Shah. In their first attempt they failed, but a year ago while the Shah was worshipping in the most holy place of the mosque, he became the victim of a fanatic Bobe, who had disguised himself as a woman. This Bobe, while under disguise, shot the king, who died two minutes afterward. Some thought that the government would again persecute them, but there were some hindrances which would not permit this. In the first place their religion is kept secret; it is impossible to know who belongs to this new sect. Secondly, many of the high classes and royal officers belong to this sect, and for this reason it would be impossible to persecute them. Thirdly, their number to-day would reach two hundred thousand, and to kill this immense company would certainly damage the government. Their antagonism against the government and against orthodox Mohammedanism is caused entirely by the lack of freedom of religious worship.

They are very warm friends of the Christians, placing in them the greatest confidence, sometimes they will even lodge in the houses of Christians, and eat with them without questioning. This a strict Mohammedan would never do. They readily allow the Christians to preach to them and to discuss religion with them. Yet it is not an easy matter to convert them, for one must know their manner of life and religious doctrines to successfully meet their arguments. A few, however, have been truly converted. This filled the Mohammedans with hatred both against the Christians and the converts. When the Christian shows the superiority of Christ and of His doctrine over that of their prophet Bobe, they are forced into silence. They are now securing many converts from Mohammedanism, and it is believed that the time will come when religious toleration will be obtained by them. This will also give the Christians a good opportunity of preaching the Gospel.

CHAPTER II.

THE KURDS.

THE Kurds are the wildest tribe of nomads in all Asia. They have been known in Europe as raiders for a long time, and during the past two years they have attracted the attention of the civilized world by their horrible massacre of the Armenians. It may be of interest to the reader to know something more of the life of this tribe. A former student of the writer, who spent several years among the Kurds as a physician, and who mastered their language and is intimately acquainted with their lives, manners and customs, has kindly given some of the information that follows.

In regard to their ancestry, it is very difficult to trace back to the original stock from which they came. They have lived under the authority of several governments, and it is believed that in their blood is a mixture of old Assyrian, Chaldean, Babylonian and Arabian. It is supposed that some of the wildest characters in all of these old nations formed the tribe of Kurds, of whom there are to-day about 4,000,000. Their dwelling place is in the Kurdiston mountains, a large territory through which runs the boundary line between Turkey and Persia. Most of it lies in Turkey. The Kurds are nominally

KURDISH CHIEF AND ATTENDANTS.

subjects of these two countries, but practically they are a band of outlaws beyond the control of any government. Those who live in the mountain districts pay no taxes to Turkey or Persia, but those residing in the villages of the plains are required to pay taxes the same as other citizens. Great numbers of them residing in the mountains and deserts are nomads, traveling where they will with their herds and flocks. A Kurd is very wild and independent in spirit. He would rather live in a cave under a projecting rock and be unmolested, than to dwell in a palace and be subject to higher authority. Some of the tribes have a small village in the mountains, to which they return in winter.

Recognizing the wild and daring spirit of these men, the Sultan of Turkey has trained some of the dwellers in villages of the plains for cavalrymen, and called them the imperial cavalry. Mounted on splendid Arabian horses and provided with modern firearms, they are well nigh invincible. The Persian government has no confidence in the Kurds, and so employs none of them in the army.

OCCUPATION.

The Kurds seldom cultivate the soil, but keep herds of cattle and horses and flocks of sheep, moving from place to place in search of good pasture. They can make very good carpets and other articles of wool, which they sell to Persian and Turkish merchants. Some of them become very rich from their herds and flocks and from the sale of carpets. One of their principal occupations is robbery. Parents teach their children how to become successful thieves. A father will give his son, of six or seven years of age, a pistol, dagger and shield and then play robber with the child, showing him how to use these deadly instruments. A Kurd once told the writer of his timid son. The child was afraid to steal. The father wanted to make him a successful thief, and so tried the following plan: The first night he sent the child to steal grapes from his own vineyard; the second night corn from his own crib; the third night, grapes from a stranger; next a chicken, then a sheep, then to enter a house, and so on, until the youth became one of the most daring of highway robbers. Then the father was proud of his son and told him that he had become a man and could marry. The girls of these tribes will not marry a man until his reputation as a successful robber is established. They want to be assured that they will not be allowed to starve after marriage.

As before stated, the Kurds are divided into

tribes, each tribe having a chief. These tribes are generally enemies with one another. The chief of a tribe will lead his men against another tribe and kill all the men and take the flocks, herds and all other property as booty. But they do not harm the women and children. An old man is not honored by a tribe. They say he can't fight nor rob and is good for nothing but to feed sheep. The man most highly honored is the one who has killed many men. When a man is killed in battle or while robbing he is honored at the funeral by the singing of many songs, in weeping and in lamentation; but not many tears are shed when one dies a natural death.

They are very skilful horsemen, and have fine horses, which become very intelligent under training. Their horses bring a high price in Turkey and Persia.

THEIR CHARACTER.

The Kurds are very quick-tempered. A slight offence will make one an enemy, and he will at once seek revenge. They are very fond of fighting and war. Very active and nimble in climbing mountains and in running and fighting. They love to revile an enemy, and are continually trying to invent new and more severe expressions of hatred. It is their nature to quarrel and fight. Brothers often become angered over a small matter and fight to death. They think no more of killing a man than we do of killing a chicken. They are very licentious, especially those living in towns and cities. Husband and wife are not loyal to each other and this is frequently the cause of murder.

As a people they have no foresight, having no thought for the morrow. They have a saying among them, " God will be merciful for tomorrow." They are very rash, acting on the impulse of the moment, and having no consideration for consequences. They never forget a kindness shown them. If a Kurd eat bread given him, he will never try to rob the giver. This is against their law. They treat travelers very kindly who may come to their tents or caves, and will offer him food. But it would not be well for him to show any gold while there, as they would follow and rob him. The most prominent characteristic of the race is thieving. Most all of the thieves in Persia and Turkey are Kurds. A Kurd was once arrested in Persia for stealing and a hand was cut off as punishment. Soon after he was again arrested for the same offence, and the other hand was cut off. The third time he was found stealing and arrested. There being no other member of the body left which is used in the art of stealing except the head, that was cut off. Thus the poor Kurd's career ended.

HOUSES.

Their houses are made of stone and mud, and are usually under projecting rocks or in the side of a hill. The roof is so low that a man cannot stand erect. The writer once visited a Kurd's home. The wife brought a carpet and spread it in the centre of the large room, on which to be seated, and then prepared some bread and milk for a luncheon. In one corner of the house were tied a pair of fine horses; in another stood several cows quietly chewing their cuds, while a few sheep were lying on the opposite side of the room. It is needless to say that this house, like all other Kurdish houses, was a dirty, filthy place. The men are tall and slender, with very black hair and eyes. Living a wild out-door life, they are very healthy and strong. The women are very beautiful. Sometimes Persian lords marry them. The food of the Kurds consists of milk, butter, bread, honey, vegetables and but little meat.

RELIGION.

In religion the Kurds are Mohammedans of the Turkish faith. Their chief priests are called

Sheikhs, and are honored as gods. They kneel before a chief priest and kiss his hands, clothes and shoes, and ask for his blessing. To penitent ones he promises that he will ask God to forgive their sins. He has absolute power over laymen. They believe his words as inspired truth and obey implicitly. One leader of this type assisted Turkey in a war against Russia some years ago. He commanded about 100,000 Kurds. He told them not to be afraid of the big cannon that would be seen when they met the Russians, for, he says, " I have by the help of Allah bound the mouths of these cannon and they can't hurt you." Believing this statement, the Kurds wildly flew into the face of the big guns, and many thousands were slain.

There are priests of different rank, but all are subordinate to the Sheikh. They are more superstitious and fanatical than the Mohammedans of Turkey or Persia. They have no written languages. They speak a mixed language collected from Persian, Arabic, Syrian and other tongues. The Kurds have been called wild asses of the desert, thirsty to shed blood and eager to plunder.

PART V.

CHAPTER I.

THE NESTORIANS.

NESTORIUS was a Greek, born in the latter part of the fourth century, near Germanicia. He became a monk in the Roman Catholic Church, and was ordained an elder by the patriarch of Antioch. Being learned in literature and an orator of power, he became patriarch of Constantinople in 428. Cyril, patriarch of Alexandria, was jealous of Nestorius, as he desired to become patriarch of Constantinople himself. He attacked the teachings of Nestorius, claiming that he taught that there are in Christ two distinct persons and two natures; and that he denied the divinity of Christ in refusing to call the virgin Mary the mother of God. This criticism of Nestorius's teachings is without foundation, as he did not teach anything of the kind. Many writers of church history have made this mistaken criticism. There are now in the possession of prominent Nestorians manuscripts of Nestorius from 600 to 900 years old, and in none of them is that doctrine held. Nestorians of to-day resent this doctrine as being no part of their belief.

Nestorius believed that Mary was the mother of Christ and that Christ had two natures, perfect God and perfect man, united with each other, but not mingled. He rejected pictures and statues representing Christ, Mary or the saints. Upon this basis he was anathematized in the council of Ephesus in 431 A.D. In the council his friends were absent and Nestorius refused to attend, as his enemy Cyril presided at the council and had power to rule it. Nestorius then united himself with the Syrian church, whose doctrines agreed with his own. He soon became a prominent leader among this sect, and the name Nestorians was given to the sect by enemies. Many learned men in the Syrian church of to-day are not willing to be called by this name. Not because they reject any of Nestorius's doctrine, but because they say it is not right for a nation to be called after the name of a stranger. But most uneducated people glory in being called Nestorians. The true origin of the Nestorians was in the old Assyrian nation. The Assyrians were descendants of Arphaxad, the son of Shem.

THEIR PLACE.

They originally dwelt in or near the cradle of mankind, in eastern Messoptomia, Assyria and Syria. At times their empire extended nearly to Babylon and Nineveh, and the great empire of Assyria was established.

LANGUAGE.

All Assyrian scholars believe or suppose that the original language spoken before the confusion of tongues was Assyrian, while some other scholars believe it was the Hebrew language. It is believed that in time it will be generally agreed that Assyrian was the original language. It is evident that Abraham was a descendant of Aber, grandson of Arphaxad, third son of Shem. The Assyrian language was spoken in purity until the time of Abraham. When he left his parents by command of God to dwell in Canaan and Egypt, it is an inevitable truth that Abraham spoke the language of his Assyrian parents. But when he dwelt in Canaan and Egypt his speech became mixed with words of those languages. The Old Testament was written by this confused language of Assyria and Egypt, which was called holy language. Therefore we see names in the Old Testament both of Assyrian and the mixed language of Abraham.

CHAPTER II.

THEIR HISTORY.

ST. THOMAS and St. Bartholomew, from the twelve apostles, and the St. Eddi and St. Maree, from the seventy apostles, have been called the apostles of Assyria. Their first patri arch was St. Maree, whose residence was in Ktis-pon, on the river Tigris, which was for a long time capital of the Sassanides dynasty. St. Maree expired in A.D. 82. After his death his disciples went to Jerusalem and chose Abriz as their patriarch. He served from A.D. 90 to 107. After Abriz, from A.D. 130 to 132, Abraham, a relative of the apostle James, became their patriarch. His successor was James, a just man, and a relative of the Virgin Mary, mother of our Lord. Akhad Abowoy became their patriarch from 205 to 220. During this period there was a severe war between the Romans and Persians. The latter then ruled over Persia, Assyria and Babylonia. The patriarch of Jerusalem, a subject of Rome, advised the Assyrians, who were under the Parthians, to elect a patriarch who was a subject of the Parthians. The Parthians ruled over Persia from 220 B.C. until 226 A.D. In all the changes of government the Assyrians have kept in office a succession of patriarchs even to the present time. The residence of their first patriarch was in Ktispon, and since that time at various places, as Baghdad, Babel, Nineveh, Mosoel, and for a long time at Elkosh, the town of the prophet Nahum. He now resides in Kurdiston mountain, in the village of Kudshanoos. His home is located on a hill surrounded by much beautiful scenery. The church in which Marshimon administers is called St. Ruben, a building made of granite.

CHAPTER III.

CLERGY.

THE Assyrian Church believe they have an apostolic succession from St. Thomas and St. Bartholomew. There are seven orders in the clergy. The patriarch, metropolitan, episcopas, archdeacon, elder, deacon and reader.

The first three are forbidden marriage. The eating of meat is prohibited; but fish, butter and eggs can be used. In olden times the presence of twelve metropolitans was required at the ordination of a patriarch, but to-day they require only four metropolitans and a few episcopas. The patriarch ordains the metropolitans and episcopas and these in turn ordain the lower clergy. It is the duty of the patriarch to overlook the entire church. Much of his time is also taken up in sending messages to Kurdish priests and to Turkish officials about wrongs that have been committed against his people. The patriarch is highly respected, and his messages receive prompt attention. His income consists of a small annual fee of five to twenty cents from all the men who belong to his sect. Fifty years ago it was a custom for elders to marry a virgin and not a widow. This custom is not observed now. They have seven orders of monks. In ancient times these were the strength of the church. The monks are pure men and learned. There are a few nuns, one of the most faithful of whom is a sister of the present patriarch.

NESTORIAN ARCHBISHOP.

CHAPTER IV.

Churches and Ordinances.

THEIR FAITH.

THEIR faith as it is described in some ancient MSS. about 500 years old, was entirely evangelical. They believed in the trinity—God the Father, Son and Holy Spirit, three persons, equal in power and nature, working together for the salvation of mankind. Some western historians have made the error of stating that the Assyrians deny the divinity of Christ or believe that He has two personalities.

From the beginning until the present time they have believed in the merit of saints. Their clergy does not claim the power to forgive sins. They accept the creed of the apostles and it is recited by the clergy and by religious men. Many days of fasting are observed, as fifty days before Easter, twenty-five days before Christmas, and others. On these days old people take no food until noon. In times of persecution their schools and books were destroyed and the people became ignorant. Catholics introduced among them their literature which changed prevailing doctrines.

THEIR CHURCHES.

Many of their churches are built of stone, while others are made of brick and clay. Some of the buildings are 1,300 years old and will stand many years to come. The walls are about eight feet thick at the base, gradually tapering toward the top. In the older churches the doors are quite low, and it is necessary for a man to stoop in entering. It is believed by some that the doors were built in this way that the church might be used as a place of refuge, rolling stones in the doorway after entering. Others say the object was to prevent horses, cattle and other animals from entering. These churches are regarded as most sacred places and are called houses of God. There is an interior stairway leading to the roof, which is necessary for repairing the roof or shovelling off snow. The yard in front of a church is shaded with elm trees; the yard is used as a graveyard. Extending from each corner of the roof is a pair of horns from a wild goat, which is a sign of sacrifice. There is a small room in the rear of the building which is called the most holy place. In this room the priests carry on certain ceremonies and no other people are allowed to enter it at any time. Before this room is a small pulpit, on which are placed a cross, Bible, and other ceremonial books. The only windows are a few small openings just below the room. Candles are burned during hours of service to light the room, and incense is burned as a ceremonial and to produce a 'pleasing odor. There are no pictures on the walls, but there are some decorations in the way of finely embroidered silk towels brought by some of the worshippers. Reading Scripture and prayer-book, and chanting Psalms are the main features of worship. There is no music except a number of small bells on the walls which the worshippers ring as they enter the building. The audience sits on the floor or stands through the service.

Assyrians believe the two chief ordinances are the Lord's supper and baptism. The ordaining of priests and marriage are ordinances that rank next in importance.

Baptism is administered by bishops and elders. All the children of a member are baptized by immersing three times. Some believe that baptism regenerates a child, while others say it will have a good effect provided the parents give the child proper training thereafter.

The Lord's supper is administered with much ritual on festival days, such as Easter, Christmas and Ascension day. This ceremony is more highly honored than any other ordinance, as it commemorates the death and victory of Christ.

Both wine and bread are used. A few years ago (and even now in some places) it was a custom to make the bread and wine from gleanings brought in from the fields and vineyards by virgins. This was considered pure and more acceptable, as it had belonged to no man. They do not believe, with the Catholics, that the bread and wine become the flesh and blood of Christ, but they put much emphasis on these ingredients after the same have been consecrated. They are then holy.

On the night previous to communion day, the priest and deacons go to the church shortly after midnight, and, entering into the most holy place, make the bread for use on the next day. The priest himself kneads the dough. This bread is considered more sacred than that made in the ordinary way. After the bread has been made, the remainder of the night is spent in chanting psalms, Scripture and prayer-book. An hour before sunrise the people flock to the church. When the church is full of worshippers the priest mounts the pulpit, chants the sacred words for an hour or more. The audience remains in perfect silence until he reaches the end of a psalm or the end of the service, when all the people say "Amen." The priest and a deacon stand in the pulpit to administer the sacrament. Communicants come forward one by one, and the priest puts a small piece of bread in their mouths, and the deacon gives the wine. Children under seven years of age do not partake of the sacrament. On these occasions the priest and deacon wear long white robes of silk or cotton, tied about with a long silk girdle. A turban is worn on the head.

CHAPTER V.

ASSYRIAN OR NESTORIAN COLLEGE.

THE golden age of this Church was the period from the fourth to the thirteenth century. They had twenty-five flourishing colleges. The most important schools were located at Oddessa, Nesibis and Urhai. The latter was called the queen of schools. These schools, while they flourished, were the secret of the Church's strength. The instructors were the most learned men of their age. Aiwaz and St. Basil of Nesibis and Urhai were among the most learned teachers. The Assyrian, Arabic and Greek languages were taught classically. Medicine, astronomy and mathematics, including geometry, were taught. Especial attention was given to the study of theology. There were as many as

2,000 monks and students in some of these institutions. Their doctors of medicine were given high positions under the Arabian and Persian governments. Literature in the eastern languages was rich. From these schools came great church fathers who defended the Church from the heretics of the age. There is one MS. 900 years old in the library of the Presbyterian Mission which is called "Persecuted Simon." It was written by Simon, a student in one of these colleges. It contains twelve lectures, all against the heretics of his age. During that period about 700 such MSS. were written. There are to-day in Europe many MSS. written by these scholars that are from 300 to 1,500 years old. The New Testament was translated into the Assyrian language in the middle of the second century. These MSS. are skilfully executed and show the beauty and antiquity of this Church. Only three of these ancient MSS. are now to be found in Persia, but there are many of them scattered in the libraries of Europe.

ܡܛܠ ܕܐܢ̈ܫܐ ܕܝܢ ܡܫܒ̈ܩܐ ܐܚܪ̈ܝ ܠܐ ܡܫܟܚ
ܐܠܗܘܬܗ. ܠܡܬܚܙܝܘ ܠܗ. ܐܠܗܘܬܗ ܓܝܪ ܒܪ̈ܢܫܐ
ܒܚܫܡ ܐܠܗܘܬܗ. ܕܡܫܝܚܐ ܕܢܦܫܗ ܒܪ̈ܢܫܐ
ܟܠܗܝܢ ܡܕܝܢ̈ܬܐ ܐܬܚܙܝ. ܒܗ ܒܐܝܩܪܗ ܕܝܠܗ
ܗܘ ܡܪܢܐ. ܘܡܫܝܚܐ ܕܡܢ ܥܠܝܐ ܫܘܒܚܗ
ܐܬܪ̈ܢܐ. ܢܦܫܝ ܢܨܠܐ ܥܠ ܬܠܝܬܝܘܬܐ ܠܟ
ܢܦܫܝ. ܐܠܗܘܬܗ ܕܡ ܡܫܝܢܐ ܠܐ ܡܬܦܪܫܐ
ܒܫܠܡܘܬܐ ܕܗܘ ܐܒܐ ܦܢܘܢ ܐܚܪܢ
ܢܘܪܘܗܝ. ܢܦܩܘ ܒܪ ܟܠ ܗܝܡܢܘܬܐ ܐܠܗܘܬܗ
ܘܟܠ ܐܝܬܝܘܬܐ. ܘܠܐ ܡܫܬܡܥܘ ܟܠ ܠܠܟ
ܘܠܐ ܟܠ ܢܒܝܘܬܐ. ܠܐ ܢܬܒܥܝ ܡܫܟܚ ܐܢܫ
ܒܪܝܬܐ. ܐܠܐ ܡܫܬܡܥ ܚܝܠܗ ܕܡܫܡܫܢܝܢ
ܐܠܗܐ ܟܠ ܕܡܬܟܫܦܝܢ ܟܠܢܫܐ ܗܘ ܕܡܬܟܫܦ
ܘܐܬܠܝܢ ܕܪܘܚܝܢ ܟܠܢܫܐ ܗܘ ܕܪܘܚܝܢ. ܫܡ ܕܗ
ܕܟܠ ܐܝܬܝܘܬܐ ܫܡ. ܡܫܡܫ ܚܝܠܐ ܟܠ ܕܢܦܫ
ܘܠܚܫܝܫ ܚܝܠܐ ܕܡܫܡܫܢܘܬܐ ܘܕܚܝܠܢ
ܘܩܕܝܫ ܩܕܝܫܘܬܐ ܕܫܡܫܐ ܕܢܦܫܗ. ܕܟܠ
ܘܠܐ ܡܦܩ ܐܠܗܐ ܠܪܘܚܐ. ܐܠܐ ܠܐ ܠܢܦܫܗ
ܕܢܦܫܗ ܟܠܗ ܡܠܟ ܡܫܝܚܐ. ܗܘ ܕܗܘ ܡܫܬܒܚ
ܐܒܘܢ. ܕܐܝܟ ܚܠܦ ܫܡܝ ܘܐܝܟ ܕܡܫܬܒܚ ܫ
ܐܒܝܢܐ ܒܫܡܗ ܢܦܫܗ ܕܟܠ ܗܘ
ܢܦܫܗ ܚܕ ܠܚܕ ܘܚܕ ܚܕ ܠܚܕ. ܐܡܝܢ

ܕܐܦ ܫܒܚܝܢ ܐܠܗܘܬܗ.

The manuscript from which this engraving is copied is from a New Testament written on deer skin by a Syrian monk 720 years ago. It is written in Ancient Syriac or Aramaic, the language in which our Lord preached His message. It begins with 1st Thess., 4th chapter. It was saved from fire among other MSS. in times of persecution. MSS. contemporary with this are found in the British Museum and in the Vatican at Rome.

Any Professor or Librarian desiring to purchase the original of this cut will please write to the author.

CHAPTER VI.

ASSYRIAN MISSIONARY SPIRIT.

THE aim of the schools mentioned in the preceding chapter was to educate monks to become missionaries and spread the Gospel. These schools were fountains from which flowed living waters for a thirsty land. There was no other nation in their age that possessed such a spirit of Christian vitality. Zeal for the spread of the Gospel was burning in their hearts as a divine flame. There was a class of bishops appointed by their leaders to awaken and keep alive this missionary spirit. "The dying love of Christ for sinners" was the text from which they preached. Also His last commission to His disciples, Matt. 28 : 19, 20. These bishops preached with an inspiration from God, and enflamed many hearts until they were ready to sacrifice their lives for Christ. These missionaries wore sandals on the feet, carried a staff of peace in the hand, and a knapsack on the shoulder containing bread and manuscripts of sacred writing. Thus equipped, they journeyed into heathen lands, following the command of their Nazarene teacher. The Church was very poor and had no board of foreign missions to guarantee even a small income. The missionaries went forth trusting in their heavenly Father. If He took care of the birds of the air, how much more would He care for the heralds of His Gospel. The week before departure was spent in fasting and prayer and consecration. On the last day they partook of communion from the hand of their leader, and solemn advice was given by the bishop. In parting the bishop kissed the missionary's brow, and the latter kissed the bishop's hand; and the bishop would say: "The Lord God of the prophets and apostles be with you; the love of Christ defend you; the Holy Spirit sanctify and continually comfort you." Some of the missionaries went to distant lands, requiring eight to twelve months to make the journey on foot. They worked in China, India, Tatariston, Persia, Bloogistan, Afghanistan, and northern Africa. Success followed their work. In the territory between China and Tatariston, they converted 200,000 heathen. Not long ago a monument was unearthed in China which had been set about 600 years ago by one of these pioneers of the cross. On it were engraved the names of many of their leaders, and also the creed, doctrine of the Trinity, and incarnation of Christ. They established twenty-five churches in northern Persia. In southern India is a small church planted at that time. These followers are now called the disciples of St. Thomas, and sometimes their young priests come to Persia to be ordained by the patriarch, who resides in the Kurdiston mountains. This spirit which was shining as the sun in heaven, began to languish in the tenth century, and by the fourteenth century had entirely died. At that time some of the Church's true sons in lamentation said: "How are the mighty fallen, and the weapons of war perished!" Hundreds of their missionaries had become martyrs of Christ in a heroic spirit. They would enter fire singing praises to God, believing their shed blood would be the seed of the Church.

CHAPTER VII.

THEIR PERSECUTIONS.

THIS ancient Church of the Assyrians, which began with the apostles, has been praised in all the eastern and western churches for its zeal in spreading the Gospel, but at no time in its history has it been free from persecution. Like the burning bush of old, this Church has been burning with persecution, but has not been consumed. The ten plagues of Egypt have been here repeated several times. It has passed through the agony of blood, but with a spirit of submission to the will of God who rules over all the changes of a nation for the good of His own kingdom. Severe persecutions began in A.D. 325. When Constantine convened the Nicean Council of the 100 delegates from the Eastern Church, mostly from Assyria, only eleven of them were free from mutilation in some form. At the time the Sassanides dynasty ruled over Assyria. Their patriarch was St. Shumon, son of a painter. No other Assyrian patriarch was equal to him in piety, integrity, and his heroic spirit of martyrdom. He was patriarch from 330 to 362 A.D. In that period the king of Persia was second shafoor of the fire-worshippers.. The fire-worshippers believed in two creative powers, Hurmizd and Ahramon. Every good thing as virtue, success, long years, praise, truth, purity, were created by Hurmizd; while wickedness, hate, war, disaster, etc., issued from Ahramon, their creator. Shafoor worshipped clean creatures of Hurmizd, such as sun, moon, and fire. Christianity was strong then, some of the royal family being Christians. The Christians were antagonized by the fire-worshippers because they rejected the sun and moon and defiled fire. Other objections were that the Christians taught that God had become incarnate and come to earth; and also that they preferred poverty to wealth and did not marry, thus diminishing the strength of the nation. The emperor issued an edict that those who would not worship the sun and the moon should pay a large sum of money. The patriarch answered that, "while God is the creator of the sun, we cannot substitute the created for the creator. Concerning a fine, we have no money to pay your lord the sum required, as our Lord commanded us not to lay up our treasures on earth." Then the king commanded that all Christians be put to death by terrible torture, except the patriarch. Him he would spare to the last, that he might be moved by the torture of others and worship the sun. But St. Shumon meantime was urging the Christians to stand firm in the faith. The king requested that the patriarch and two chief bishops be brought before him. It had been a custom to prostrate himself before the king as a token of honor, but on this occasion he wished to avoid any show of worshipping a creature, and did not prostrate himself before the ruler. The king asked him to worship the sun. St. Shumon replied: "If I refuse to worship the king, how can you expect me to worship the sun, a creature without life?" Being unable to make him worship the sun, the king put him in jail for the night. Next morning the patriarch was taken before the king again. On his way he met a steward of the king, who was a Christian, but had been worshipping the sun to please the king. St. Shumon rebuked the steward for being faithless. The steward was touched by this rebuke, and, going before the king, confessed that he was a Christian and must, therefore, be beheaded. But he requested that a herald be sent through the streets to proclaim that he had been a faithful subject to his ruler, and that he must die because he was a Christian. This was granted.

In company with one hundred bishops and priests, St. Shumon was brought before the king. Again he was told that he could save the life of himself and his people by worshipping the sun. St. Shumon replied, "We have one God and Jesus Christ our Saviour as the object of our worship. Our Lord teaches us to be faithful to kings and to pray for them, but we are forbidden to worship any creature." Then the king commanded that all of them be beheaded next day. The night in a dungeon was spent in prayer and song and words of advice from St. Shumon, in love and tears of sorrow. The patriarch consoled his followers by referring to the fact that St. Paul and the apostles spent many nights in prison. He said, "The prison is heaven, because the presence of our Lord is with us. This is our last night on earth; to-morrow we will be crowned." Taking the New Testament in his hand, he preached to his condemned disciples of the suffering and death of Christ, and then administered the Lord's supper. At the close of his prayer he thanked Christ that they were worthy to be His martyrs, and further prayed, "Watch with me, O Lord; help our infirmity. The spirit is willing, but the flesh is weak. Thanks be to God that we are to become martyrs on the same day of the week as did Christ." In the morning he, with his 100 followers, stood before the king. The bishops were first beheaded, and St. Shumon spoke to each one as follows: "My son, close your eyes, and after one minute you will be with Christ." St. Shumon had asked to be beheaded first that he might not see the death of his beloved followers, but he was not heard. At last came his turn, with two chief bishops. When he alone was left he sang a song of thanks to God that out of 100 martyrs not one had denied the faith. His song was as follows: "Praised be Thy power, our God; let the kingdom of our Saviour be victorious. Thou quickener of life, Thou hast prepared a crown for Thy martyrs." Then he was beheaded with an axe.

Another severe persecution was in the 14th century by Tamerlane. In 1848 two Kurdish dukes Baddirkhunback and Nurullaback and their armies came whirling down from the Kurdish mountains, and in one month massacred 25,000 Assyrians. The spirit of martyrdom still lives in this people, as was shown in 1893, when two men and a girl were killed as martyrs. No doubt they are to-day singing praises before the throne of God, hundreds of martyrs from this nation.

CHAPTER VIII.

THEIR CONDITION AT THE TIME AMERICAN MISSIONS WERE STARTED.

THE colleges of the Assyrians were destroyed four hundred years before the American missionaries came. Not a single school was left, and the only effort at education was by monks teaching dead languages to aspirants for the priesthood. Learned bishops and monks who were full of the spirit of Christ in spreading the Gospel at home and abroad had all vanished. Some of the clergy could not understand what they read. Priests and their parishes became blind to the Word of God, as their books had been burned in times of persecution by the Mohammedans in order to keep them ignorant. Sometimes there was only one priest in a dozen villages. The clouds of ignorance spread over all the nation. Their sun went down. Regeneration and conversion were unknown to them. Traditions prevailed among priests and laymen. They trusted in saints and in ancient and holy church buildings. In their ignorance they offered sacrifice to martyrs and built tombs to prophets; put more hope in the merit of fasting than in Christ. A small number of New Testament manuscripts, which were written in dead languages were used only in taking oaths. Sometimes laymen kneeled before them and kissed them instead of obeying the truth that was written in them. The candlestick of the church was turned down and the light quenched. Moreover the Mohammedans had threatened to massacre them if they did not accept that faith. The Assyrians had lost about all of their Christianity except the name. Among 100,000 Christians in Kurdiston and 60,000 in Persia there was only one lady who could read, and she was a nun, sister of the patriarch. The words of the daughter-in-law of Eli when she said, "The glory is departed from Israel," could have been applied to this nation.

PART VI.

CHAPTER I.

INTRODUCTION OF MISSION WORK.

WHILE the sky of Persia was covered with heavy clouds of ignorance and even the dim ray of light in Assyria was almost quenched, suddenly God, in His great wisdom and wise providence, awakened the consciences of godly men in America to think about mission work in Persia. In the year of 1832 Messrs. Smith and Dwight were sent by the A. B. C. F. M. to examine the degenerate and antique Churches of the East. They travelled through Syria, Asia Minor, Armenia and Persia. In the latter country they remained in the city of Oroomiah for several weeks, and met the bishops and leaders of the Assyrian Church, with whom they visited the villages of Assyria. Men, women and children everywhere greeted them with great joy. In this way they became acquainted with the needs of the nations. Mr. Smith said at that time: "I see that this field is white and ready for the harvest. In all my journey I have seen no people as willing to accept the Gospel as are the Assyrians of Persia. It is a good field for the work."

On their return to America Messrs. Smith and Dwight reported the needs of the Assyrians and their readiness to accept the Gospel. But the question arose, Where is the man qualified for the work, who can overcome the difficulties? In the beginning of every great work there must always be a unique man to lead it. God found only Moses among all the Israelites as being competent to bring His people out of Egypt. He elected George Washington to make free America. Even so, in His providence he found the Rev. Justin Perkins to be the man equipped for this great mission work. In 1835, Justin Perkins and Dr. Grant as his medical assistant, were appointed to the work in Persia. These two blessed messengers of Emmanuel shone in the dark skies of Persia, and I believe will everlastingly shine in the sky of heaven.

They were received by the natives as if God had sent them from heaven. Many Assyrians went out to meet them with tears of joy in their eyes. Perhaps some one will ask why the Assyrians were so eager to receive the missionaries. Were they awakened to their spiritual condition? The answer is, they were not fully awakened to their great need of spirituality, but they were eager to be saved from the wicked plan of the Mohammedans to convert them to that faith by force, if need be.

CHAPTER II.

METHOD OF WORK.

MR. PERKINS gained the confidence and won the love of the people by making himself one of their number, by adopting their customs and speaking of Assyria as "our nation." In this way he got very close to the people, they believed him their friend, and were not afraid to come near to him. In adopting the native dress it must be remembered of him that he wore the hat commonly worn by aged religious men. It was made of sheep-skin and was not less than two feet high.

The Assyrian churches were open to the new missionaries and they preached two or three times every Sunday. There was marked interest in the new teachers from the beginning, and every service was attended by 200 or 300 natives. In addition to the observance of Sunday the Assyrians have numerous sacred or saints' days; at such times the churches are better attended than on Sundays. Services were also led by the missionaries on these days. Through every day of the week the missionaries were busy scattering the blessed seed. When there were no services held in the churches they would meet in some private home. Several neighboring families would come in, and all would listen to the Gospel. The writer remembers when he was a boy of Dr. Coan lodging at his father's home several nights and holding meetings. Our homes were very humble among the Assyrians. The houses were low and dark, blackened with smoke from the ovens. The floor was covered with cheap mats, but some people had a carpet, which was spread when guests came.

Most of the families are very large, numbering from ten to thirty-five. In many instances, five or six sons having married, are found raising their families under their father's roof. The food for all is cooked in the one oven, but more than one table is used when the family is very large. The meals set before the missionaries were very different from what they had been accustomed to. There were no knives and forks, no tables and chairs. But the missionaries humbled themselves, sat on the floor, and ate of the poorly cooked food with their fingers.

In summer most of the people were working in the fields and vineyards. The missionaries would visit them at their work and ask permission to talk for an hour. The workers would gather in the shade of a tree and for an hour listen to the message. Many times these meetings proved very beneficial. In 1843 the well-known Fidelia Fisk, and several other noble women, came to work for women. They would visit them in their homes or where they were at work in the field or vineyard, and while helping them in their work would strive to ennoble their lives by talking of Christian principles.

A story is told of a missionary who one day passed a shepherd among his flocks. He asked the shepherd if he ever prayed. The reply was that he did not know how. When the good man offered to teach him the shepherd said it was useless to try, as he could not learn. But the faithful missionary was eager to teach truth, even to the dullest minds, and so began teaching him the Lord's prayer. But the shepherd could not memorize it. Remembering how this shepherd knew every sheep in his flock by name, a happy thought struck the missionary. He would name a small number of the sheep with words or phrases of the Lord's prayer. Calling the sheep and giving them these new names the shepherd soon learned the prayer, and could repeat it readily.

When passing that way a few weeks later the missionary asked the shepherd if he still remembered the prayer. Calling his sheep, the herdsman went through the prayer with but one mistake. The missionary complimented him, but told him that he had omitted "forgive our sins." "Did I?" replied the shepherd, "Oh, I know how it happened. "Forgive our sins" took sick and died a few days ago." This made it necessary to point out another sheep and name it "Forgive our sins." Missionaries have to resort to various methods to teach truth. Many times the hearts of parents are won by the missionaries kissing one of their beloved children. They proved to the people that they were not ashamed to be as brothers to them. This kind of treatment will touch the human heart in any clime.

CHAPTER III.

DEVELOPMENT OF MISSION AND ORGANIZATION OF THE CHURCH.

AFTER several years' work by Justin Perkins and Dr. Grant, his medical assistant, the mission had grown until more workers were needed. From time to time other workers came, such as Messrs. Stoddard, Stakings, Dr. Coan and Mr. Rhea. The latter was known among the natives as the prince of preachers. He died in that country and his widow, Mrs. Rhea, now resides in Lake Forest, Ill. Other workers who should be mentioned are Dr. Larabee and Mr. Cochran.

During these years of preaching, seed was sown for more thorough work. Revival meetings were begun in the churches, and, in answer to prayer, the Lord poured out His Spirit upon both preachers and listeners. At some of these meetings there would be from thirty to one hundred men and women crying aloud and trying to learn what they must do to be saved. In those times some of the penitents, in their ignorance, prayed prayers that they would to-day be ashamed of. One old man, who is now an elder, became terribly in earnest when he was under conviction and was seeking conversion.

In his anguish he prayed thus: "O Lord God, Father of Christ, send Thy Spirit and regenerate all of this church. If you won't do this, then destroy this church over our heads and kill us." This prayer, and others like it, was prayed with such intense earnestness, that another seeker nearby thought the Lord would answer it at once; and so, reaching for his hat, he prayed: "O Lord, don't do this until I get out; then destroy all of them if you want to." Hastily uttering this prayer, he sought safety outside the walls of the building. When the old elder was recently reminded of the prayer he made years ago, he was not ashamed, for he said that was all they knew in those days, as they had not yet learned how to pray.

Until the time of these revivals there had been no separation of the missionaries from the old Assyrian Church. It had been their custom to take of the Lord's Supper from the hands of Assyrian priests. Mr. Cochran, president of the Oroomiah College, thought it was now time to form a separate organization. Accordingly the new converts were organized into a separate church on evangelical principles.

This separation aroused the bitter opposition of the bishops and priests of the old Church for a time, but it finally resulted beneficially to both sects. The ancient Church tried to attract and hold the people by adopting the same kind of preaching and Sunday schools as were being carried on by the evangelical branch. Preaching sermons was a new work for priests of the old Church, and many amusing mistakes were made at first. One priest in an enthusiastic discourse, when intending to call the Mohammedans dogs, made the sad mistake of addressing his audience as, "Ye dogs and sons of dogs." At another time a bishop having announced that he would preach a sermon, carefully wrote his discourse. A large and expectant audience greeted him. When it was time to deliver the address the bishop felt in every pocket for his written sermon, but failed to find it. Turning to the audience, he said: "Satan, the accursed, has stolen my sermon out of my pocket and disappeared with it." Being unable to make the address from memory, he dismissed the audience.

The Church has developed along this line, however, and to-day in Oroomiah their services differ very little from that of the evangelical churches. Once a tiny rivulet, the evangelical Church has become a brook which flows in beauty and waters much of a thirsty land. It is the hope of Persia.

The statistics of mission work in Persia in 1895 were as follows: Five presbyteries, fifty-five churches, 2,600 members, 4,000 Sunday-school scholars, 4,500 attendants at preaching services. These five presbyteries make one synod. Besides this there are two other presbyteries with about 500 church members. There are seven missionary stations, viz., Oroomiah, Tabriz, Tehron, Salmas, Hamadon, Myandab and Moesul. These are in charge of American missionaries; besides them there are many native preachers in the different towns and cities. Oroomiah is the mother station. Most of these missions are dependent on missionaries, but some of them are self-supporting. The total number of Protestants in Persia will number fully 15,000.

CHAPTER IV.

Religious Education.

COLLEGE.

THE first need of the nation was a college. In 1836 Justin Perkins gathered a small number of deacons and priests to teach them for the work of spreading the Gospel. The native priests were very ignorant, but Mr. Perkins believed it would take fewer years to prepare them for the work than children, so he opened a rude school in a cellar. At that time the priests in common with all other people drank wine and were frequently drunk. When Dr. Perkins opened his school for the native priests and deacons many of them brought a bottle of wine for use during school hours. Dr. Perkins dealt patiently with them, but stated that it was against the rules of the school to bring wine. They replied that they would not come to study if they were not allowed to bring wine. So wine they brought. One native preacher, who is now an old man and a fine singer, told at a recent synod of this early school, of which he was a member: One day they got too much wine and went upstairs and began to dance. Dr. Perkins called to them and asked them to dance a little slower. They replied to the teacher that they would dance slower, but kept on dancing. In time the habit of drinking was left off and total abstinence was firmly established.

The school in the cellar has grown until now we have in Oroomiah a fine brick building in which the college classes meet. In it are six branches; high school, preparatory, college, medicine, industrial and theological. Its superintendents from the start have been able men. Dr. Perkins founded it, Mr. Cochran further developed it, and the late Dr. Shedd, a profound theologian, contributed his fine ability to the institution. Several Eastern languages are taught. Mathematics, including algebra and geometry, geography and history are taught, but of course not as completely as in America.

LADIES' SEMINARY.

When the missionaries came to Persia there was only one woman among the 200,000 Assyrians who could read. Girls were not encouraged to study, as it was against the law and believed to be useless. This belief originated in Mohammed's teachings. Fidelia Fisk, soon after her arrival, saw the condition of the women and determined to open a seminary. At first it was difficult to get girls to attend. If mothers were asked to send their girls, they replied: "What is the use? They can never become bishops or priests." If a girl was asked to attend she would reply that she did not have time, as she must be preparing a dowry for her wedding, an event that would certainly occur before her eighteenth year. However, a small free school was opened for girls, where the branches taught were similar to those of the college. Fidelia Fisk labored faithfully in her duties as teacher and made for herself a lasting reputation in that country.

Her patience was often severely taxed. It is told of her that once after she had become old she was trying to explain an example in multiplication, when a loose tooth dropped out of her mouth. She sank wearily into a chair, exclaiming, "It's no use; there is no god of mathematics in this nation."

There stands to-day on the same site where this faithful soul started the little school, a beautiful brick building known as the Fidelia Fisk Seminary. It is also self-supporting, and is attended by 75 or 100 students. Now the girls and mothers laugh at their old superstition about education, as they have learned that it prepares one for something besides bishop or priest. Fathers want their daughters to attend the seminary, and young men who are looking for a wife appreciate the importance of the training which seminary girls have received. They know that she can raise their children better, keep the home cleaner, and better understand her relation to her husband.

While the seminary was founded by Fidelia Fisk it was developed largely by Jenny Deane, who was superintendent of the institution for thirty years. It was under her direction that the building was erected. Miss Deane was a very wise lady, and has few, if any, superiors in America in the management of an institution. As a retired missionary she now resides in Detroit, Michigan. She will never be forgotten by the many women in Persia whom she has so greatly helped. There are also four other seminaries in Persia for ladies.

MEDICAL SCHOOLS.

The beauty and blessing of medical mission work will be better understood if we contrast it with prevailing ideas about medicine. Until about fifteen years ago there were no Persian doctors who had become such from the study of books on medical science. There were, however, many quack doctors who had a system of superstition which had been taught them orally by older men. Blades of some kinds of grasses which are known to medical science as having no medicinal properties, were the chief remedies prescribed for disease. Internal diseases were called supernatural, and it was believed they were inflicted by evil spirits. None of the doctors could do anything for this form of disease, as they considered it out of their realm. A patient with an internal disease was sent to the priest, who would diagnose the case by looking into the Koran or some other book in which he locates the particular demon that is afflicting the patient. Writing something mystical on two slips of paper, the priest gives direction for their use: " This one soak in a cup of water and have the patient drink the water. The other, bind on the patient's arm. I find that it is demon so and so that is afflicting the sick man, and I have bound the mouth of that evil spirit so that he cannot do further harm.

There are several remedies for fever. One is to tie seven knots in a white thread and fasten it around the wrist. Wearing this fifteen or twenty days cures the fever, they say. Another remedy is to remove the clothing and jump into cold water before breakfast. If a man has a severe attack of colic and cries, "I die, I die," his friends run for the nearest bald-headed man, as he is known to have power to remove the pains by firmly pressing the smooth surface of his cranium against the surface of the patient's body nearest the seat of pain. Many bald-headed men in other countries laugh at this remedy, but Persian doctors affirm that it will cure, and that skeptics should try it. Pork is never used as food, but it is believed to remove rheumatism when bound on the parts afflicted.

There are now some medical men in Persia who have graduated in an American or European medical college. Patients for whom they have prescribed often consult the Mujtahid before taking the medicine. Once a man with a diseased foot came to Dr. Cochran for treatment. The doctor told him that his life could be saved by amputating the foot. The patient consulted a Mujtahid, who told him that it was against religion to part with any member of the body. Therefore the patient retained his foot and died. The modern midwife is greatly needed in Persia, as many women die for want of attention, and it is against the law for male doctors to give them treatment. The name hospital was unknown in Persia before the missionaries came. But, thanks to God, we have today three missionary hospitals. The good they do cannot be expressed in words. They are open for all, no matter what their beliefs. The largest one is in Oroomiah. It is under the charge of Dr. Cochran, a godly man, who is known in all Persia. The late Shah appreciated his work so much that he gave him the highest degree that is possible to give to a foreigner. When patients enter these hospitals, lie down on clean beds, are given good food and kind treatment, they are surprised, and sometimes have said that heaven cannot be a nicer place. Some wild Kurds have been brought to the hospitals. They came in like roaring lions, but went out meek as lambs. Hundreds of people have been snatched from the mouth of the grave by treatment received here. They cure not only the body, but the soul also. Two wild Kurds who were healed here became Christians and are now active church members. Dr. Cochran has from six to ten native students of medicine. They take a three years' course, and some of them have become such useful physicians that the Shah gave them the title of count. The Mohammedans have confidence in the Christian doctors, and send for them to treat their children and wives in all cases except childbirth.

COUNTRY SCHOOLS.

There were no schools for common education among the people before the missionaries came. They met with some opposition in starting country schools from superstitious old men. They said the Europeans and Americans are a cunning people. They will fill our children's heads with notions that will take them away from us to foreign countries. On the other hand there were many parents eager to have their children get learning. So schools began. Books and writing material were so expensive and scarce for a time, that a canvas with the alphabet printed on it was stretched on the wall. Thirty or more children could stand before this canvas and study. For those who were learning to write, boxes of sand were provided. Herein written language was traced. There are to-day seventy schools for children in the district of Oroomiah. The population of this district is nearly half a million. Some of the schools are self-supporting, while in others the teachers' salaries are paid by the missionaries. These schools are like a garden of flowers in a desert. They have a very strong moral and elevating influence in a community. It is generally believed by Christian workers there that there is no better foundation for the future of the Church than these schools. In them are taught three languages, a little geography, mathematics and the Bible. Nearly all the students can repeat from memory the ten commandments, the Lord's prayer, and creed of the apostles. The chief aim is to teach the fear of God. A good many students are converted in school. After school some of the students go among their neighbors in the evening to read the Bible to them. The teachers are chosen by the Board of Education. One important rule governing the choice is that the applicant must be a regular member of the Church. The teachers are very devoted and faithful to their work. They consider that their work among the children is similar to a pastor's work among his people. They watch after their pupils in school and out as a shepherd cares for his flock. A monthly meeting is held for teachers, at which the best methods of teaching are discussed. One of the principal subjects considered is, how to develop spirituality among the pupils. These meetings are refreshing to the teachers, and they return to their work full of the love of Christ, zealous to spread His truth. Sometimes a religious mid-week meeting is held in the schoolhouse for students only. These meetings often bear blessed fruit. In one such meeting in a preparatory school over which the writer held supervision, thirteen boys of ages from thirteen to sixteen years, were converted. These boys remained after the meeting closed, and, touched with the Spirit of God, they prayed, with tears in their eyes. Some of them have since become preachers of the Gospel. In the country schools some of the teachers work more faithfully for the salvation of their pupils than pastors work for their flock. In one school two boys were attacked with a fatal disease. The teacher, accompanied with several pupils, visited the first sick boy and asked him if he was afraid to die. He replied that he did not want to give up his studies. The teacher asked if he did not know that Christ was a teacher. The dying boy was gladdened by this thought, and, with a smile on his boyish face, he said: "I'm going away to Christ and He will teach me." With these words his soul took its flight above. The other sick boy was then visited and comforted in the same way. He, too, soon died of the fatal disease. The missionaries are carrying on 113 schools in Persia and the Kurdiston mountains. The number of teachers employed is 116 and there are 1,821 boys and 720 girls; total 2,541.

TRANSLATION OF BOOKS.

When the missionaries first came to Persia, ancient Syriac was the language of literature; therefore the common people could not understand anything in the ceremonial words of the priests. Dr. Perkins, with the aid of native scholars, translated the Bible into the common language, or modern Syriac. After the new translation was printed the common people were surprised and rejoiced greatly at having the sacred Word in a form that they could understand. From time to time other books were translated, such as parts of commentaries on the Bible, Pilgrim's Progress, Rest of Saints, Morning to Morning, etc. These books are read in connection with the Bible in the daily worship of the native Christians. Rev. Benjamin Larabee, D.D., with some native scholars, greatly improved the translation of the Bible into modern Syriac, about two years ago, by a careful revision of the first translation. Mrs. J. H. Shedd, who was known as the "Mother in Israel," did a great work for our people in translating books and tracts, and in preparing the Sunday lessons.

CHAPTER V.

The Gospel and Temporal Improvement.

THE Assyrian houses were one-storey, low flat roof, and built of mud. Mohammedan law. was opposed to Christians building houses of more than one storey. The houses were poorly kept, dark and unfurnished. This was the case even when a man was well-to-do and could have afforded something better. Families were large, numbering from ten to forty. It was the custom when sons married to raise their families, for a time at least, under the parental roof. The mother or father was supreme authority in the home, but they could not always control the sons, daughters and grandchildren, and there is much quarrelling and frequently fighting. However, custom demands that a son bring his bride to his father's house. If he does not he is called mean. When the writer married his wedding ceremony was performed at the preparatory school where he was then teaching, and he did not take his bride to his father's home. He remembers that his good mother was grieved and shed tears at this breaking away from custom. Men in the street were inclined to look upon him with scorn.

The house that accommodates a large family is usually divided into several rooms. There are often four beds in one large room. The reader must understand that these large families do not give rise to immorality. Men may be wicked in other ways, but this vice is very uncommon.

Christians were compelled by Mohammedan law to wear poor grade clothing. They could not wear any garments commonly worn by lords. Men wore coarse, home-made clothing, something like American blue jeans of earlier days. Women dressed in plain cloth, usually colored red. Lords objected to their subjects wearing nice clothing. They suspected the spirit of pride was growing underneath, and might some day resent their authority. Christians were compelled to wear red braid on their clothing to distinguish them from Mohammedans. It was a sin for a Mohammedan to give the same salutation to a Christian that was given to his own sect, so it was necessary to mark the Christian's clothing. Only bishops and some few prominent men were allowed to ride a horse, while other Christians must walk or ride a donkey, for the Moslems said: "God created horses for us and donkeys for you." If a Christian, who was riding a horse, met a Moslem, he should dismount, bow to him, and remain off the horse until the Moslem had passed.

The per cent. of death in infancy was very

large. Mothers did not understand how to nourish the delicate life during the most trying period. The infants were not dressed warm enough in many instances. In other instances the clothes about the child bound it helpless and injured it, sometimes causing death. Ignorantly, they exposed them to contagious disease. Before the missionaries introduced vaccination, hundreds died with smallpox. The women of the mission have taught the natives a great deal about caring for young children, and now many a mother dresses and cares for her babe after American custom.

TEMPERANCE.

The Assyrians were a great nation for drinking wine. Many men owned vineyards and made from the fruit some of the best wine. One man was known who made 100 barrels of wine one year for his own use. Wine and not water was the drink. Grapes were very cheap, and the poor man could be supplied with wine.

Nearly all forms of industry and business were suspended in winter, and the time was spent in trying to get joy from the cup. They said wine was love and good fellowship, which is a common notion in many nations of the earth to-day. When a man had a guest from a distance, he would invite forty or fifty neighbors to his home where the entire day would be spent in eating and drinking. Next day one of the neighbors would entertain the company, and so the feast would continue for a week or more. By the end of the debauch perhaps one or more of the number would have met death. Falling by the wayside at a late hour, or tumbling from a housetop as he was journeying homeward, he would die from cold or from the shock. In those degenerate days idleness, extravagance and drunkenness were praised in a man. When such a one died, an engraving on his tombstone would show that his table was always spread and provided with wine for his friends. Many a man was brought to poverty by these habits of extravagance and drunkenness. The women were required to let wine alone, that they might cook much food for these degenerate Christians. On such occasions the master of the house demanded that the very best food be put before his guest.

The missionaries have completely broken up these customs. The evangelical church forbids its members to make or taste wine or to sit among drinkers. Any who disobey this rule are dismissed from membership. Rev. E. W. Pierre, one of the most beloved of all missionaries, spent one winter in preaching temperance. Many were converted to his views on the subject and brought their wines, many barrels, and poured it into the streets. They believed it would be a sin to even sell it. The old Assyrian Church members have given up their former ways and are now temperate. Formerly it was the glory of a man to be idle and drunken, but now public opinion has been entirely reversed. The drunkard is looked upon as an object of shame.

The Assyrians used to observe many saint's days. At times as many as four thousand men and women would gather in the yard of some building built in honor of an ancient saint, and would there spend several days in eating, drinking and dancing. Sometimes quarrelling, fighting and even murder would result from these gatherings. Moslems often mingled with the crowd and sometimes kidnapped some of their fairest daughters. Instead of places of worship, these gatherings became places of sin. All of these vicious customs have now vanished before the influence of the true Gospel.

More than half the days of the year were days of fasting with the old Assyrians. On these days they ate no meat, milk, butter, cheese, eggs or fish; some very religious old people would eat nothing before noon. All has now been changed.

Members of the evangelical Church do not fast, and but few of the old Assyrians do. There is no longer faith in the virtue of fasting.

CONVERSION TO MOHAMMEDANISM.

Before the missionaries came many beautiful girls and ladies were converted by force to the faith of Moslems. Girls were often stolen when alone in the fields and vineyards. Mothers feared for their daughters, and advised them not to wash their faces, nor put on nice clothes lest a Mohammedan would be attracted by their beauty. When a Mohammedan saw a beautiful girl he would say, "God created her for us and not for these infidels." When girls were converted by force, it was not much use to complain to the government, as the government is Mohammedan and it is in the Mohammedan doctrine that when a man converts a Christian he has done a good thing and all his sins will be forgiven. The method of making the convert is not questioned. The conversions now as compared with the number when the missionaries came are very few. Kidnapping is not easy now, as parents can telegraph to the king, or the prime minister, or even to Europe, and cause much trouble.

A few years ago a prince had a beautiful Armenian stolen from her home, and tried to get her to consent to be a Mohammedan and become his wife. But the woman stood firm, and denounced him and his faith. Her friends, and the missionaries of all denominations, were making an angry search for the missing woman, and the prince ordered his servants to return her to her native village. When a girl has been stolen and complaint is made to the government, officers bring the girl into court, if she can be found, and ask her if she had been taken by force, or whether she was willing to become a Moslem. If she says she was taken by force, she is returned to her parents. There are a few cases where women willingly go to the Moslem, but this is from their wickedness or their poverty.

MORALS ELEVATED.

Not many years ago a Moslem would enter the private homes of the Assyrians without an invitation. The husband and father did not want him there, but so long had his rights as a man been ignored that he did not have the manhood to drive him away. Then, too, he feared if he offended the Moslem, that the latter would secretly destroy some of his property. These uninvited visits gave the stranger an opportunity to become acquainted with the family, and perhaps an attempt to kidnap a daughter would follow. But this has changed. If a stranger enters an Assyrian home to-day he behaves like a gentleman or he is ordered to leave. The manhood and independence of the old Assyrian has been aroused.

In a national conference of the Protestants, Catholics and Old Assyrian Churches, held a few months ago, rules and plans for the development of the nation and the uplifting of morality were adopted. Among other things Christian girls and women are prohibited by these rules from working for Mohammedans: second, no girl nor woman can go to a city of Mohammedan merchants to do trading. This is the first conference of this kind that has been held by Assyrians for 400 years.

Many of the native young men who have been educated by the missionaries have become able men and influential citizens. There are some of them who can stand before the king and speak with greater power than any of the government officers. This is in great contrast with the condition of Assyrians before the missionaries came. In those days leading Assyrians could not stand before even a low court to plead their cause.

In 1893 a general, third in the government, visited Oroomiah college. When he saw the training of the young men he was impressed and afterwards, in a conference of lords, said: "The young men who are being educated in the mission schools would become leaders in the political affairs of our nation if they had a chance. I believe a time will come when they will hold high offices, and the sons of lords will be ruled by them unless you do something for the future of your children."

The Shah has given the title of count to some of the graduates in medicine. He sees their useful work and says they are helping his people. The royal family and some officers favor indirectly, if not directly, modern education; and they have confidence in Christians. The occupation of selling merchandise is being entered by Christians; they have much prejudice to overcome, but will likely succeed gradually.

Thanks to God, many of the old oppressions have passed away. Assyrians can now build any kind of house they want; Moslems can no longer say that they must walk or ride a donkey; they can wear clothes of any style or quality they choose. No longer are Christians required to trim their clothes in red to mark their inferiority. All these are the fruits of the blessed Gospel.

CHAPTER VI.

MISSION WORK AMONG MOSLEMS.

MISSION work indirectly and slowly spreads among Moslem. The Koran forbids Christians to preach to Moslems, and no Christian dared discuss questions of religion with Moslems before the time of missionaries. To attempt to show Christ's superiority of Mohammed was forbidden. If a Moslem should say, "Mohammed was a greater prophet than Christ. Ours is the true religion. You are infidels." The Christian, with a timid, downward look, would reply, "Yes, sir, you are right." But the answer to this assertion to-day is a firm "No, sir." The Christian now sees truth clearly and feels it his duty to uphold it. There is now free discusison of religious questions. A Christian discusses with Moslem priest if he chooses. And sometimes they call at the homes of Moslems and read the Bible to them. The Christian feels it his duty to discuss with any one who approaches him, as he possesses light which that one needs. There is in one city an evangelical church in which all of its members are Mohammedan converts, while many other churches have a few. The spirit of these converts is that of martyrs. The Koran teaches that any Mohammedan who denounces the faith deserves death, and that one who kills the deserter has done a noble deed. Some of these converts have suffered martyrdom, and one who was killed after great torture, prayed as his last words: "O Jesus, we thank Thee that Thou hast made us worthy to be Thy martyrs. Our supplication is that our blood may become as seed to Thy Church." No doubt God will answer this prayer in due time. The seed is sown; the leaven is mingled and will in time, no doubt, leaven the 9,000,000 Mohammedans.

The writer, a representative of the evangelical missions, wishes to express his deep gratitude to the American Board who started mission work in Persia, and to the Presbyterian Church, which, in 1871, assumed the responsibility of the work and has since so nobly carried it on.

www.ingramcontent.com/pod-product-compliance
Lightning Source LLC
Chambersburg PA
CBHW031736230426
43669CB00007B/369

* 9 7 8 3 7 4 3 3 1 6 8 6 7 *